THE ART OF DEATH

WRITING THE FINAL STORY

Also by Edwidge Danticat

The Art of

DEATH

WRITING THE FINAL STORY

Edwidge Danticat

Graywolf Press

This publication is made possible, in part, by the voters of Minnesota through a Minnesota State Arts Board Operating Support grant, thanks to a legislative appropriation from the arts and cultural heritage fund, and through a grant from the Wells Fargo Foundation. Significant support has also been provided by Target, the McKnight Foundation, the Amazon Literary Partnership, and other generous contributions from foundations, corporations, and individuals. To these organizations and individuals we offer our heartfelt thanks.

This book is made possible through a partnership with the College of Saint Benedict, and honors the legacy of S. Mariella Gable, a distinguished teacher at the College. Support has been provided by the Manitou Fund as part of the Warner Reading Program.

Published by Graywolf Press
250 Third Avenue North, Suite 600
Minneapolis, Minnesota 55401

www.graywolfpress.org

Published in the United States of America

ISBN 978-1-55597-777-1

2 4 6 8 9 7 5 3 1
First Graywolf Printing, 2017

Library of Congress Control Number: 2016951195

Cover design: Scott Sorenson

For Rose Souvenance Napoléon and
André Miracin Danticat, who led me here.

We die containing a richness of lovers and tribes,
tastes we have swallowed, bodies we have
plunged into and swum up as if rivers of wisdom,
characters we have climbed into as if trees, fears
we have hidden in as if caves. I wish for all this
to be marked on my body when I am dead.
I believe in such cartography—to be marked by
nature, not just to label ourselves on a map like
the names of rich men and women on buildings.
We are communal histories, communal books.

—Michael Ondaatje, *The English Patient*

Contents

THE ART OF DEATH

WRITING THE FINAL STORY

Introduction: Writing Life

My mother once gave her factory forewoman my first novel for Christmas.

"I see her reading the newspaper all the time," my mother said before leaving for work one December morning when I was twenty-five. "I'd like to give her your book."

I spent the day pondering an appropriate dedication for a woman I'd never know, except through a few details my mother had mentioned. Mary was Chinese, short, and patient.

Finally, I scribbled, "To Mary, Merry Christmas. Thank you so much for being nice to my mom."

My mother asked me the best way to tell Mary, in English, *Se pitit fi m ki ekri liv sa a*, "My daughter wrote this book."

My mother and I practiced this sentence in English many times together. *My daughter wrote this book. My daughter wrote this book.* I imagined this daughter as a child my mother and I shared, our common dream offspring, whom I called Sophie, after the tormented narrator of *Breath, Eyes, Memory*, my first novel.

Mary never said anything to my mother about my novel after my mother gave it to her. Maybe Mary didn't like fiction, hadn't enjoyed the book, or perhaps my mother's gift had puzzled her. Maybe Mary hadn't been able to decode my mother's message in giving her the book: *This is not all there is to me. Beyond the walls of this factory, I have a much bigger life. I have children and they've done wonderful things. One writes books.*

When my mother was diagnosed with stage 4 ovarian cancer in early 2014, every time we'd go see a doctor more than once, she would ask me to give that doctor one of my books. She underestimated how embarrassing it was for me to seem to be bribing someone with something that was precious to me but that they might consider worthless. I would tell her I'd do it, then we'd quickly move on to the next doctor, and the one after that, each of whom would bring us more and more dire news, until my mother no longer considered them worthy of any gifts at all.

The one doctor she insisted on—aside from my friend Rose-May, who had become her primary physician and already had my books—was her oncologist, Dr. Blyden. One day, while I was drilling Dr. Blyden with my Internet-research-inspired questions, he asked what I do for a living. I told him I am a writer.

My mother wanted me to give Dr. Blyden a copy of my 2007 memoir, *Brother, I'm Dying*, in which I describe, among other things, my mother's early years with my father, who'd died of pulmonary fibrosis in May 2005.

Instead, I gave him my most recent novel, *Claire of the Sea Light*. My mother smiled as I handed Dr. Blyden the book. She even smiled at Dr. Blyden's two observing medical students.

As he walked out of the room, Dr. Blyden looked back at my mother, and I imagined him seeing her in a slightly different light. Until then, I hadn't quite understood the power of a moment like this. A moment where your apparent value suddenly rises in the eyes of someone else, especially a person who has your life in his hands. During subsequent visits, though, Dr. Blyden never mentioned the book.

The last time my mother and I were in Dr. Blyden's office, we told him that my mother had decided to stop chemotherapy and let nature take its course.

"Tell him it's up to God now," my mother said in Creole, using me yet again as her translator.

After a long pause, the doctor agreed that at her age, seventy-eight, the type of vigorous treatment she would now need might considerably reduce her quality of life. Lingering longer than usual, Dr. Blyden told us about a patient of his who was the same age as Mom and had the same diagnosis. That patient had also decided to stop treatment after one round of chemo.

"Where is she now?" my mother asked after I'd translated this for her.

"On a cruise," the doctor said.

Dr. Blyden had told us this story, I realized, to show his support for my mother's choice, and for that my mother seemed grateful. At least that other dying woman was feeling well enough to go on with her life, I imagined her thinking.

As my mother and I were leaving Dr. Blyden's office that day, I heard him tell one of his medical students something that made me understand even better why my mother had made me a one-woman bookmobile on her behalf.

"This is a special woman," Dr. Blyden said, referring to my mother. "She raised an author."

My mother beamed. The big, broad smile on her face that day made me want to run from the doctor's office and shout, irrationally, to everyone in my path: "My mother is dying *and* I write books!"

Writing has been the primary way I have tried to make sense of my losses, including deaths. I have been writing about death for as long as I have been writing. Spoiler alert here: the mother of the narrator of *Breath, Eyes, Memory* commits suicide. (Maybe Mary's silence had something to do with that.) Dozens of people fleeing political persecution in Haiti drown, just as they did in life, in my second book, a short-story collection called *Krik? Krak!* My third book and second novel, *The Farming of Bones*, recounts the 1937 massacre in which thousands of Haitians were methodically slaughtered on the orders of Rafael Trujillo, a dictator from the neighboring Dominican Republic. While much of my work is based on actual events, I chose those particular subjects in part because, early in my life, before anyone close to me had died, I was so afraid of death that I wanted to desensitize myself to it. Now that my father and mother and many other people I love have died, I want to both better understand death and offload my fear of it, and I believe reading and writing can help.

"We die," Toni Morrison eloquently states in her 1993 Nobel Lecture. "That may be the meaning of life. But we do language. That may be the measure of our lives."

Over the years, I have read and reread many writers who have managed, and even triumphed at, the art of writing death. This is not an objective grouping but a deeply personal one. The works I discuss here are novels, stories, memoirs, essays, and poems that, both recently and in the past, I have found myself returning to when living with and writing about death. These authors have provided me with hints, clues, maps that I hope might lead me to some still-undiscovered and undefined "other side," which is often mislabeled as closure. I am writing this book in order to learn (or relearn) how one writes about death, so I can write, or continue to write, about the deaths that have most touched my life, including, most recently, my mother's.

Living Dyingly

More and more of us are writing our own obituaries. Some of us meticulous planners write a few paragraphs that we hope will be printed in our local newspaper or on our funeral programs after we die. However, most of us are creating detailed digital narratives every day, sharing images and words that will remain available long after we're gone. There are websites devoted to memorializing the dead, virtual cemeteries where our life stories continue. These days, when we say the dead are always with us, we are hardly being metaphorical. Hundreds of images of the dead, or some previous version of them, can be as close to us as the smartphones in our pockets. Facebook accounts that remain open after someone has died continue to receive messages, many of which are addressed directly to the dead.

A few years ago, an artist I was acquainted with died of lung cancer when he was in his early thirties. Each year on his birthday, he still gets a slew of new messages on his Facebook wall. People tell him how much they love him and miss him. Some of the messages make it seem as though he were traveling.

"I know you're in a better place," a family member writes, "but I still miss you."

In the past, only close relatives might have had access to notes or letters left behind in sealed boxes in attics or basements. Now everything we write online or share on social media becomes potential fodder for our eulogies or obituaries. Still, it's easier to draft a self-eulogy or obituary when one is healthy and well, when death is still an abstraction rather than a constant companion. When people are sick or dying, the act of putting together final thoughts about oneself is much more laden with emotion, and one fluctuates daily, sometimes hourly, between all five stages of Elisabeth Kübler-Ross's grief cycle of denial, anger, bargaining, depression, and finally acceptance.

My mother spent several weeks before she died recording a series of monologues on a handheld audio-cassette player she'd had for years. On the cassette, she leaves detailed funeral instructions and advice for my brothers and me on how to treat each other and raise our kids.

On the cassette, she never quite says, "I know I am dying." Instead, she says, "Be patient with your children and love them, like I loved you."

She never told me she was recording this cassette. She must have done it late at night when she was alone with her thoughts. She was possibly struggling with her fear of dying, which, to borrow from Ernest Hemingway's "iceberg principle"—in which, like an iceberg, one eighth of a narrative is clearly seen or "above water"—must have been the other seven-eighths.

"I'm not necessarily dying either today or tomorrow," she says, showing a gradual evolution toward acceptance. "But we all must die one day."

I was surprised to learn, a few years ago, that many newspapers prewrite obituaries for public figures. Though my mother was not a public person, I wish I'd prewritten her obituary while she was dying. I wish I had been courageous enough to crack the iceberg and ask her what she wanted said about her at her funeral. I suppose she might have mentioned something on her cassette if it had been that important to her. After all, she told me what kind of shoes I should wear to her wake. (No open toes.) In addition to the "iceberg," humor would have been one of my mother's tools if she were writing her death.

I don't know very much about my mother's childhood, because she never liked to talk about it. The fact that I know so little about her early life means that I will not be able to fully reconstruct her on the page. But I have already created fictional versions of my mother, taking the bits I know and morphing them into different women, some who are like I imagined her to be, some who are like I wanted her to be, and others who represent the worst-case scenario, the worst mother I could possibly have had. My mother has given birth to more women than me, and perhaps in her death she will breed even more.

After my mother died, I called her two younger sisters, my aunts Grace and Thérèse, and asked them to tell me some interesting details about her childhood that I could include in her eulogy. My aunts ended up telling me some of the few things I already knew: that my mother was the sixth of nine children, that her lifelong hobby was sewing and embroidering, and that as a young woman she made extra money by embroidering elaborate trousseaus for brides. Each time my mother designed and embroidered a tablecloth or a sheet for one of her clients, she also made one for herself, so by the time she met my father, she already had everything she needed to set up her own house. Still, I want more. I want more than my mother was willing to leave me in words. But even if my mother had also retold me these exact same things, I still wish I'd heard them again, one final time, from her.

My mother did not leave behind an obituary, but she left behind her cassette.

"I love you okay" is all she says in English, even after having lived in the United States for over forty years. The rest of the cassette is in Haitian Creole. And to me, she keeps saying, "*Met fanm sou ou.*" "Be your own woman"; "Be a strong woman."

I fill in the rest of that phrase, knowing that this is

what she must have been thinking: Be the woman I raised you to be.

When you're young, your parents can seem immortal, then they get terminally ill and they remove the possibility of either you or them being immortal. When they die, you realize what it's like to suddenly occupy an ambiguous space in the world. If both your parents, who are the people who created you, can die, then you too can die. With this in mind, you become acutely aware that we are all "living dyingly," as the writer and commentator Christopher Hitchens calls it in *Mortality*, a collection of the essays initially published in *Vanity Fair* magazine the year before he died of esophageal cancer.

"My chief consolation in this year of living dyingly has been the presence of friends," Hitchens writes. "I can't eat or drink for pleasure anymore, so when they offer to come it's only for the blessed chance to talk."

Unlike ordinary talk, which can become routine, this kind of talk is pressing, urgent. It has an expiration date, of which those who are caught up in the regular routine of life are not yet aware. My mother, I imagine, used her cassette as her own blessed chance to talk. And like Hitchens's lyrical, clever, and sometimes sarcastic essays, Mom's monologues were much more about life than death. Her blessed chance to talk, like

Hitchens's blessed chance to write, was in itself a kind of hopeful story.

We cannot write about death without writing about life. Stories that start at the end of life often take us back to the past, to the beginning—or to some beginning—to unearth what there was before, what will be missed, what will be lost. Whether we love or hate them, the people dying on the page must somehow reveal themselves to us. We must be invested in their fate, whether we want them to live or die.

The final moment of death, especially when a prolonged illness is involved, is one of many deaths, anyway. Smaller deaths precede it, including, among other things, possibly one's loss of autonomy and dignity. When faced with their own death, writers—and, in fiction, characters—develop their own lingua franca to describe their dying. That language sometimes changes as death nears, but it might also remain the same.

In *Mortality*, Hitchens never seems to waver, on the page at least, in his steadfast determination not to feel sorry for himself. Even while describing the indignities he suffered as a cancer patient, he skillfully adds some levity and humor.

"I heard a soothing and capable voice saying, 'Now you might feel just a little prick,'" Hitchens writes.

"(Be assured," he adds: "Male patients have exhausted all the possibilities of this feeble joke within the first few days of hearing it.)"

I can almost see him smirking as he writes this. Dying is not taking everything away from him. The core of his personality is still intact: his intelligence, his sarcasm, his sense of humor. Though this is not true of everyone who is dying, at least it is for him and he wants us to know it. He wants his readers to realize that he's still hanging on, that he's still there.

Both in lifestyle and tastes, my mother was the complete opposite of Hitchens. He was an atheist and she was deeply religious. "God is good" was her mantra. *God Is Not Great* was the title of one of his most popular books. Everyone who came to visit my mother while she was sick, including her minister of forty years, who traveled from New York to Miami to see her, was told, "God sent you." The one thing Hitchens and my mother did have in common, though, was that neither one seemed too interested in what Joan Didion, in *The Year of Magical Thinking*, calls "the question of self-pity," or in asking themselves, "Why me?"

Hitchens in *Mortality*

To the dumb question "Why me?" the cosmos barely bothers to return the reply: Why not?

Mom after a chemo session

I am almost eighty years old. I don't have small children. Why not me, instead of some young woman with babies?

"I don't *have* a body, I *am* a body," Hitchens writes.

A body that, in my mother's case, shortly before she died, had to have feces extracted from it by hand, and blood-tainted fluid pumped out of it via her belly, every few weeks.

"There is a river inside me," my mother would say half-jokingly, "and it never stops flowing."

We are all bodies, but the dying body starts decaying right before our eyes. And those narratives that tell us what it's like to live, and die, inside those bodies are helpful to all of us, because no matter how old we are, our bodies never stop being mysterious to us. Many of us don't pay much attention to our well bodies. Our sick bodies and the sick bodies of our loved ones become our obsessions. We have no idea how one part— the brain, for example—might be functioning so well, while the rest of the body is failing. How can one lung or kidney be diseased and the other one be perfectly fine? It is perhaps the act of defending separate parts of the body that eventually kills the entire organism.

In her 1989 book, *AIDS and Its Metaphors*, Susan Sontag writes of that book's 1978 predecessor, *Illness as Metaphor*, that she didn't think it would be useful to write "yet one more story in the first person of how someone learned that she or he had cancer, wept, struggled, was comforted, suffered, took courage . . . though mine was also that story."

She did not want to share deeply personal experiences that because of their common occurrence had become hackneyed, as even death can become a cliché. So Sontag drew on stories that had already been written, including Leo Tolstoy's novella *The Death of Ivan Ilyich*, and she wrote her own book, "spurred by evangelical zeal as well as anxiety about how much time I had left to do any living or writing in."

That zeal goes along with a chronicler's persistent desire to share, and a sense of gratitude for that blessed chance to talk.

In *The Cancer Journals*, poet and activist Audre Lorde sees many parallels between the fourteen years she spent battling breast cancer and the other struggles she'd had throughout her life as a black feminist, lesbian, mother, and "warrior poet."

Even while comparing her mastectomy to the way the Amazons of Dahomey chopped off their right breasts to become better archers, she still mourns her intact body.

> I want to write of the pain I am feeling right now, of the lukewarm tears that will not stop coming into my eyes—for what? For my lost breast? . . . For the death I don't know how to postpone? Or how to meet elegantly?

Both Lorde and Sontag set out goals for their "living dyingly" texts. Maybe this has something to do with the urgency of their mission. There's no time for exposition or warm-up, just a vital task to be completed.

How does one prepare to meet death elegantly? And what if there's no elegance to be had, especially if one is being ravaged by pain, or is losing control of one's limbs or bowels? Is our job as writers the same as that of caretakers? As writers, we might seek the least elegant death possible for our characters, while we would want our loved ones to die "soft as cream," as Toni Morrison writes in *Beloved.* That tension has been most elaborately explored by dying writers who, like Hitchens, Sontag, and Lorde, have had that blessed chance to write.

After her mastectomy, when she couldn't write, Audre Lorde recorded on cassette tapes her thoughts on mortality and other issues.

> In playing back the tapes of those last days in the hospital, I found only the voice of a very weakened woman saying with the greatest difficulty and almost unrecognizable: . . . *I don't want this to be a record of grieving only. I don't want this to be a record only of tears.*

Lorde is admonishing herself, even in her weakest state. Though she has become both a writer and a recorder of a dying body, she does not want to write only of loss and grief. She doesn't want to make dying the central story.

Four months after my mother died, I realized while rereading *The Cancer Journals* that I was the same age that Audre Lorde was when she had her first mastectomy.

"I am 46 years living today and very pleased to be alive, very glad and very happy," she writes on that birthday.

Reading this somehow reassured me that one could indeed "live dyingly." Or die livingly. At least on the page. After all, to die, to echo *Peter Pan*, can be "an awfully big adventure." As the father of the essay, Michel de Montaigne, writes, "Dying . . . is the greatest work we have to do," yet we can't get good at it by practicing, since we experience it only once. Death also cannot exist in isolation, even when someone dies alone. Death announces itself in the middle of a life being lived, in media res.

"There is no such thing as a natural death," Simone de Beauvoir writes in *A Very Easy Death*, her account of the final weeks of her mother's life, "You do not die from being born, nor from having lived, nor from old age. You die from *something*. . . . Cancer, thrombosis, pneumonia: it is as violent and unforeseen as an engine stopping in the middle of the sky. . . ." Or we die of death, as Gabriel García Márquez has written: death, which he once referred to as "the only important thing that happens in a lifetime." Dying, especially prolonged dying, is rarely passive or monotonous. Dying people are engaged in the most significant battle of their lives. Dying is not, as Tolstoy puts it in *The Death of Ivan Ilyich*, "a case of the appendix or the kidney, but of life . . . and death."

The act of writing, or talking about one's death, makes one an active participant in one's life. Those who write, or make cassettes, about dying are not dying passively, so we should not write about them that way. Even their final surrender, if it ever comes, is a hard-won process. Whether young or old, dying people are not usually expected to submit but to fight.

It is not surprising that Dylan Thomas's almost century-old poem "Do Not Go Gentle into That Good Night" is so often invoked when we talk about the dying. We might be tempted to whisper a few lines from that poem into the ears of our loved ones as they lie comatose in intensive care or spend their final days in hospice.

> And you, my father, there on that sad height,
> curse, bless, me now with your fierce tears, I pray.
> Do not go gentle into that good night.
> Rage, rage against the dying of the light.
>
> And you, my mother, there on that sad height . . .
> Did you rage enough?

We like to think that our loved ones didn't surrender too quickly. It might comfort us to know they at least tried to put up a fight, if not for their own sake but for ours, just to have one more hour, one more day, one more week, one more month, a few more years with us.

On my mother's cassette, I heard some ambivalence. She did not want to die ("I'm not necessarily dying either today or tomorrow"). But she eventually came to terms with the fact that she might ("But we all must die someday"). Still, she was not willing to rage, to fight until her final breath. Otherwise she would have chosen the second, harder course of chemotherapy.

While we, her children, generally respected her wishes, one of my brothers disagreed with her about stopping the chemotherapy. My mother had taken care of our father when he was terminally ill, and our father would have jumped at any opportunity to live a few more years. She was not going to live a few more years, my mother countered; she had only a few more weeks of prolonged suffering. Rather than fighting it, my mother embraced the dying of the light.

One of the sympathy cards I received after my mother died had a Lucille Clifton poem pasted inside it. The mother of the friend who'd sent me the poem had also recently died. The poem was called "oh antic God."

oh antic God
return to me
my mother in her thirties

The hymnlike, staccato, pleading start to this poem immediately brought tears to my eyes. "Oh antic God," I wanted to scream, "return to me my mother from the day she was born. Give her another beginning and not an ending."

My mother at thirty-four was giving birth to me in Haiti. Then two years later she gave birth to my brother Bob. My mother at thirty-eight stayed behind in Port-au-Prince with my brother and me after my father moved to New York to look for work. Then she left us with my uncle Joseph and his wife, Tante Denise, to join my father in New York, when I was four. My mother in her late thirties was an undocumented immigrant living in Brooklyn, away from her two small children. She was a factory worker who made handbags for pennies on the dollar. My mother in her early forties had two more children, my brothers Kelly and Karl.

In Haitian Creole, when someone is said to be *lòt bò dlo*, "on the other side of the water," it can either mean that they've traveled abroad or that they have died. My mother at forty was already *lòt bò dlo*, on the other side of the water.

Ars Moriendi

When my father's youngest sister, my aunt Rezia, died, in Haiti, she had outlived my father by seven years, something she marveled at each time I saw her after his death.

"I can't believe I'm still here and your father's not," she would say in the same pained voice in which she recounted burying her two oldest sons, a few years back.

The day Tante Rezia had a massive stroke, she had just closed the stall in downtown Port-au-Prince where she'd been selling books and school supplies for over thirty years. She was on her way home when she stumbled and fell. The last two words she uttered were to a fellow vendor: "*Tèt mwen.*" "My head."

I heard about Tante Rezia's fall and eventual coma the following morning at 3 a.m., after she was hospitalized in a trauma facility near the Port-au-Prince airport. My cousin Agathe, who was one of many family members keeping vigil, called to ask if I would speak to the visiting American doctor on call.

The doctor was a youthful-sounding woman from Philadelphia. Tante Rezia had been unconscious since her fall. She'd suffered a hemorrhagic stroke due to her high blood pressure. Tante Rezia's prognosis, the doctor said, was very poor. Agathe had been warned by another doctor that Tante Rezia might not live through the night. The visiting doctor would neither confirm nor contradict this during our conversation.

"Sometimes the body takes its time," the doctor said.

Tante Rezia's body did take its time. Though she never regained consciousness, she remained in the coma for another week before she died.

If Tante Rezia's death had been fictionalized, there probably would have been a deathbed scene. Being in Miami, over seven hundred miles away, I tried to imagine one.

Before my mother died, I had only "witnessed" deathbed scenes in literature and film. Other ideas about a person's final moments had come from stories I'd been told about death, including my father's.

Were Tante Rezia's final moments like Sula's in Toni Morrison's eponymous 1973 novel of female friendship? What kind of pictures drifted through Tante Rezia's mind before she took her final breath? Did she feel tired, an exhaustion so profound that it "barely let her open her lips, let alone take the deep breath necessary to scream"? Did she think that on the other side of her death would be an endless sleep, a much-needed rest? Was she amazed that dying didn't hurt as much as she thought it might?

THE ART OF DEATH   25

> While in this state of weary anticipation, she [Sula]
> noticed that she was not breathing, that her heart
> had stopped completely. A crease of fear touched her
> breast, for any second there was sure to be a violent
> explosion in her brain, a gasping for breath. Then
> she realized, or rather she sensed, that there was not
> going to be any pain. She was not breathing because
> she didn't have to. Her body did not need oxygen.
> She was dead.

Notice the precise use of the limited third-person point of view here. We are inside Sula's head, one might even say her heart. She's stopped breathing, but the definitive moment, at least for me, is not the death itself, which is stated simply enough ("She was dead"), but the "crease of fear" that touches her breast, then eventually goes away.

The crease precedes the grand terror that Sula has been expecting, "a violent explosion in her brain." Both the crease and the potential explosion capture the extremes of Sula's unpredictable personality, which Morrison evokes one final time through Sula's forward thinking. Sula's realization that her body no longer needs oxygen is not sad but triumphant, as if needing oxygen were one more weakness she's shed by dying. We also get to experience a few moments past Sula's last breath, to the threshold of whatever might come next.

"Sula felt her face smiling. 'Well, I'll be dammed,' she thought, 'it didn't even hurt. Wait'll I tell Nell.'"

As this eternally smiling face indicates, death is neither the end of Sula's story, nor the end of her complicated friendship with Nell. "Wait'll I tell Nell" shows that those two will never be done with one another. They're still going to be in touch, even though one of them is no longer on this earth.

For many of us who have watched loved ones die, it is a matter of both deep curiosity and concern as to when they will finally accept that they're dying. I have tried to pinpoint that moment on my mother's trajectory. Was it when she started making the cassette? Or was it during that final weekend, when one of my brothers, the one who thought she should continue the chemo, was visiting her from New York? She told him she was thirsty, but each time she tried to swallow a mouthful of water, she choked on it, so my brother got her an orange Popsicle, which the hospice nurse had recommended. My mother looked blissful as she licked half the Popsicle, and while handing the rest to my brother she said, "I feel like I'm slipping away." "*M santi m prale.*" Then she motioned toward him with her hands and made the gesture of a bird flying away.

It is, I learned over the course of my mother's gradual decline, impossible to watch someone you love die and not feel the encroaching brush of death upon yourself. It's as if death had entered the room, paused, then moved past you before laying its hands on your loved one. So it's true, you realize: we're all eventually going to die, though some of us might die sooner than others.

In *Confession*, a short memoir, Leo Tolstoy writes about some of the deaths that affected him. He saw fellow soldiers die in the Crimean War. He witnessed a beheading at an execution in Paris. He watched his brother die of tuberculosis. Five of his thirteen children died. His mother died when he was two years old and his father when he was nine. All of which might have led him to conclude that "one day sickness and death will come (and have come) to my loved ones, to myself, and nothing will remain but stink and worms."

Perhaps Tolstoy needed to be in that particular state of mind to write so vividly and consistently about death. In *Confession*, he recalls a fable about a traveler who jumps into a well to escape a wild beast. At the bottom of the well is a dragon waiting to tear the traveler to bits. Trapped between the wild beast and the dragon, both of which will kill him in an instant, the traveler grabs a shrub growing in the crevices of the well and holds on for dear life. The traveler then realizes that two mice are nibbling away at the stem of his shrub. Death, the traveler concludes, is inevitable. Then he notices two drops of honey on the shrub's leaves and begins to lick them. Trapped between the beasts of life and death, that honey is all we have at any particular moment, Tolstoy seems to be saying. And toward the end of one's life, there might not be pleasure even in licking a few drops. (Or, in my mother's case, an orange Popsicle.)

"Those two drops of honey . . . my love for the family and for writing which I called art—are sweet for me no more," Tolstoy writes.

Tolstoy's near-suicidal despair is palpable in that book, and I'm not recommending that one try to replicate it for the sake of art, but it's evident in both *Confession* and *The Death of Ivan Ilyich*, as well as his novels, that Tolstoy could write so well about death because he was fascinated by it and could easily imagine himself dying.

Having been exposed to death does help when writing about it, but how can we write plausibly from the point of view of the dying when we have not died ourselves, and have no one around to ask what it is like to die?

"Death," as Michael Ondaatje writes in *The English Patient*, "means you are in the third person."

Even taking into consideration "near-death" narratives, we have no true accounts of the most common type of death, the irreversible kind. In the end, we can only imagine what it's like to die, and to stay dead. ("The reason for living is getting ready to stay dead" the dying—or already dead—Addie remembers her father saying in William Faulkner's *As I Lay Dying*.)

"In reality there is no experience of death. . . . it is barely possible to speak of the experience of others' deaths. It is a substitute, an illusion, and it never quite convinces us," Albert Camus writes in *The Myth of Sisyphus*, his treatise on his philosophy of absurdism.

Still, we continue to speak of other people's deaths, as Camus did in his novels and essays. We write about the dead to make sense of our losses, to become less haunted, to turn ghosts into words, to transform an absence into language. Death is an unparalleled experience, so we look to death narratives, and to the people in our lives who are dying, for some previously unknowable insights, which we hope they will pass on to us in some way. Someone's calm and dignified death is meant to be a model not just for the way we might eventually want to die, but also for the way we might want to live. Someone's tortured and melodramatic death is supposed to be a cautionary tale, a warning for us to put our house in order so that we might do better, or be better, when our turn comes.

In *The Writing Life*, novelist and memoirist Annie Dillard exhorts us to write as though every story were our last, as though we were dying. "At the same time, assume you write for an audience consisting solely of terminal patients. That is, after all, the case. What would you begin writing if you knew you would die soon? What could you say to a dying person that would not enrage by its triviality?"

Every writer brings a different set of beliefs, experiences, and observations to their writing about death. Tolstoy's desire to share with others what it's like to die apparently extended beyond literature. He supposedly came up with a series of codes, including eye movements, so that when his time came, he could describe to the people around him what it was like to die. Tolstoy wished for a singular death and he eventually got one. At eighty-two, he died of pneumonia in the stationmaster's house at a small-town train station. Some of his final days were recorded on film, and his last words were said to be "How do peasants die?"

How *do* peasants die? Or how do mothers die? Even when we're there to witness a physical death, we're not 100 percent sure. Each death is as singular as the individual who is dying, and in the end we will get no definitive answers. Lacking absolutes, all we have is our faith and belief and imagination to either haunt or comfort us.

There's also no limit to how long a death scene can last. In Taiye Selasi's 2013 debut novel, *Ghana Must Go,*

Kweku Sai, the family patriarch and a gifted surgeon, spends over ninety pages dying in a garden in his native Ghana. His death begins on the first page with "Kweku dies barefoot on a Sunday before sunrise, his slippers by the doorway to the bedroom like dogs." He takes his last breath ninety-one pages later.

In between are flashbacks to crucial moments from Kweku's life in both Ghana and the United States, ranging from childhood memories to how he met both his wives, the birth of his four children, and the death of his mother. To mirror the stop-and-go urgency of Kweku's "slow-building" heart attack, some of Kweku's thoughts flow like stream-of-consciousness poems. A few simply drift into micro paragraphs.

In the garden where he will die, Kweku thinks in alliteration. His thoughts have both a poetic and a musical quality.

Glittering garden.
Glittering wet.

As he lingers there awhile, he realizes:

Dewdrops on grass.
On the soles of his feet:
sudden, wet, unexpected, so shocking they hurt.

Time is rendered in shorthand.

Winter again, 1989.
The delivery ward at the Brigham. . . .

And, later,

A hospital again, 1993.
Late afternoon, early autumn.
The lobby.

Borrowed from screenplays, this abridged method of marking place and time is quite fitting given that Kweku imagines his life as a kind of reality show in which a cameraman is shadowing him to record different versions of the man he's trying to be: the considerate husband, the well-respected doctor, the provider father. This type of shorthand is necessary also because Kweku knows he has very little time left. In a reversal of Hemingway's "iceberg," Kweku's abundant, multi-layered "spiral of thoughts" is guiding him toward accepting death, but not before he revisits as much of his life as he can. His recollections also highlight the fact that he's spent his life focused on the wrong things.

"I didn't know *what was beautiful,"* he thinks; *"I would have fought for it all, had I seen, had I known!"*

This is the biggest regret of this dying man's life, and

Selasi wants to be certain we don't miss it, amid the beautiful and powerful imagery that follows, many pages later.

>   And so to death.
>
>   He lies here facedown with a smile on his face. Now the butterfly alights, finished drinking. A spectacular contrast, the turquoise against pink. But unconcerned with this, with beauty, with contrast, with loss. It flitters around the garden, coming to hover by his foot. Fluttering its wings against his soles as if to soothe them. Open, shut. The dog smells new death and barks, startling the butterfly. It flaps its wings once, flies away.
>
>   Silence.

One might be tempted to call out the butterfly as an easy metaphor for death and the afterlife. I have used it myself, as has the maestro Gabriel García Márquez, as a symbol of visiting spirits, a sign of mystery, and a harbinger of good and bad news. In *Ghana Must Go*, the butterfly is so intimately woven into the story that the metaphor does not feel forced.

The butterfly makes its first appearance at Kweku's mother's wake, where, "Black and blue . . . an almost neon shade of turquoise," it lands on his mother's toe.

Later, as he is dying, Kweku's mother's voice is one of the last things he hears—she tells him to "rest"—so it's not surprising that she would also return to soothe the soles of her son's feet, just as some ancestor had done for her, via the butterfly.

Selasi gives the Sais their own singular butterfly, a swordtail, which has the specific task of preparing members of a migratory family for their final journeys.

The way words are laid out on the page in *Ghana Must Go* also creates an emotionally charged linguistic and emotional map. The word "Silence," for example, gets its own page in the novel, making that page look like a tombstone. Selasi's "Silence" is also a transitional narrative break between the first section, "Gone," in which Kweku dies, and the second section, "Going," in which his family comes together to bury him. I also think of this page as an equivalent of the moment right after somebody has died when others have yet to be notified. In that moment, in that silence, the dead person is still alive in many people's minds, which makes it tempting to delay breaking that spell.

A few years after reading *Ghana Must Go*, I couldn't stop thinking about the book, especially as people in my life were dying, both those who lived close to me and those who, like Tante Rezia, lived far away. I wanted to find out how Selasi came to write Kweku's death so convincingly, so I sent her an e-mail.

She wrote back that she'd written the first hundred pages of her novel "in a sort of frenzy, more quickly than I'd written anything to date. I heard the first sentence, ran to my laptop, and didn't stop typing." Looking back, though, she could see that a kind of intricate structure had emerged: episodic, achronological.

> The common trope is one's life flashing before one's eyes. As Kweku lies dying, moments from his life flash before his eyes (and ours), an image or sensation in the present moment triggering a memory from the past. The dewdrops in his garden remind him of the birth of his daughter. One memory follows on naturally from another, much in the way the mind wanders: forward and backward, gently circling the present. He is dying, yes, but he is remembering the heartbreaks that have shaped his life. Kweku's final heartbreak—less tragic than triumphant—is discovering that he was loved. He has found a worthy "point" to his story. In this, for me, he dies redeemed.

Tante Rezia's deathbed scene, I'm told, was mostly unremarkable, at least from the outside. She remained unconscious in the hospital, but was on oxygen and IVs for a week. Her two sons and other family members took turns keeping vigil at her bedside. One afternoon my cousin Fritz heard a loud crackle, as though she were clearing her throat. It also sounded like she'd been running too fast and was trying to catch her breath. Then her chest stopped moving up and down and there was no more breath.

From the inside, it might have been different. Tante Rezia might have been thinking about the sudden events that had precipitated her toward death, the uncertainty of deeds left undone and words left unsaid. She might have been drafting in her mind sentences she would never get to say to her children and grandchildren. She might have been worried about her stall, her pens and paper, as well as her books, her livelihood for the past thirty-five years. She loved the books she sold: textbooks and occasionally some French novels. She loved their smell, their shapes, and the noise they made when their spines were cracked. Maybe her final thought was of this one concentrated pleasure: the ecstasy of unpacking books.

Was she afraid to die? Apparently, the older we are, the less afraid we are to die, no matter what our belief system. Tante Rezia was seventy years old and a Christian. She might have been praying, either to live a few years longer or to painlessly slip away.

Tolstoy too was a Christian. *The Death of Ivan Ilyich* echoes the principles of *Ars Moriendi*, a fifteenth-century guide that taught Christians the proper way to die. In the *Ars Moriendi* tradition, before the dying take their final breaths, the deathbed becomes a battleground between good and evil spirits, and between the present and the past.

"Is there any meaning in my life that wouldn't be destroyed by the death that inevitably awaits me?" Tolstoy wonders in *Confession*.

We may never fully be able to answer that question, but the structures and demands of a life—or a story—urge us to at least try.

Peabody, the rural doctor in Faulkner's *As I Lay Dying*, offers what I consider a plausible, if not direct, reply to Tolstoy's question.

> When I was young I believed death to be a phenomenon of the body; now I know it to be merely a function of the mind—and that of the minds of the ones who suffer the bereavement. The nihilists say it is the end; the fundamentalists, the beginning; when in reality it is no more than a single tenant or family moving out of a tenement or a town.

I know now, having watched my mother die, that death is a phenomenon of both the body and the mind—her body and mind, and now mine too. I believe that death is not the end. I'd rather think that it's some type of new beginning, a positive one for her. I like to think as well that it's like moving from one place to another, a more beautiful and peaceful place, a more permanent tenement or town.

We like to think of dying as being most comforting when it's not a solitary affair, as it was for Kweku Sai. Saying that someone has died alone is like stating that that person has received an even graver sentence than usual. But what if the last face a person sees is that of the person who is taking her life away?

I read Alice Sebold's *The Lovely Bones* when it came out, in 2002. It was the book everyone was talking about that year, and for good reason. The novel is narrated by a dead girl, who tells in great detail the story of her rape and murder and its aftermath, from her version of heaven.

After a brief prologue, the novel's first chapter begins:

My name was Salmon, like the fish; first name, Susie.
I was fourteen when I was murdered on December 6, 1973.

This is testimonial prose, right down to its apparent verisimilitude. Exact dates and other concrete details of the period create the feel of an eyewitness account, albeit one that's being told from beyond the grave. Susie Salmon doesn't even have a proper grave, we come to find out as she narrates her own death.

THE ART OF DEATH   39

Alice Sebold makes some courageous narrative choices, the most audacious being the prolonged death scene in which Susie's neighbor Mr. Harvey rapes, kills, and dismembers her. I can't recall ever reading a murder scene—at the beginning of a book, no less—that is as unflinching yet also as filled with life: the life we are about to mourn, the life that's slowly being carved away, piece by piece, from this young girl. Susie Salmon's prolonged killing proves what Hospital Tommy, an old barber, declares in Toni Morrison's *Song of Solomon*, that "every killing is a hard killing."

"Killing anybody is hard," he continues. "You see those movies where the hero puts his hands around somebody's neck and the victim coughs a little bit and expires? Don't believe it, my friends. The human body is robust. It can gather strength when it's in mortal danger."

Susie's is certainly a hard killing, an unbearably hard killing. Susie fights as much as she can, yet Mr. Harvey eventually overpowers her. Her killing, she tells us, took place at a time "when people believed things like that didn't happen." She also tells us other things. She describes the scent of cologne that invades the air as Mr. Harvey approaches, the earthy smell of the hole in the ground, the eerie light in there that "would make his features hard to see when he was on top of me." She tells us too that she was a member of the Chess Club at school and that she liked a quote from the Spanish poet Juan Ramón Jiménez, which is in her junior high school yearbook. It turns out that the quote contains great advice for writers as well: "If they give you ruled paper, write the other way." No ruled paper here. Alice Sebold is writing the other way.

Susie's descriptions of her murder make for an agonizing read. Still, as Susie matter-of-factly describes fitting her limbs back together in heaven, Sebold convinces us that there is no other way her story could have been told.

"A good sentence in prose should be like a good line in poetry, unchangeable," Gustave Flaubert once wrote in a letter to his lover, the poet Louise Colet. This is also true for a powerful scene, or series of scenes, in a novel. A great scene should be unchangeable. Susie Salmon, to use Faulkner's words, is "a single tenant" moving out of this world in the most brutal way, with her unchangeable memories—her shadows—trailing behind her.

Sometimes we must write what we are most terrified to write, and we need our shadows, however haunting they may be, in order to write the best book we can. In February 2003, Alice Sebold told *Boston Globe* reporter David Mehegan, "That idea of a shadow that travels with you, that has another destiny than you might have imagined, has always fascinated me. For me, that shadow has always been a teenage girl who died."

Soon after I finished reading *The Lovely Bones*, I was curious about Sebold's other work and sought out her 1999 memoir, *Lucky*. *Lucky* recounts in unwavering detail Sebold's brutal rape in a Syracuse, New York, park when she was a college student. *Lucky* is as unflinching as *The Lovely Bones*, even more so because we know that the assault and torture Sebold endured actually occurred. After her rape, Sebold was told she was "lucky": a girl had recently been murdered and dismembered in the same tunnel, in the same park.

Sebold's memoir offers some interesting insight into her fiction, just as *Confession* allows us to probe the mind that created *The Death of Ivan Ilyich*, *Anna Karenina*, and Tolstoy's other works. Sebold started writing *The Lovely Bones*, then realized she couldn't finish Susie Salmon's story until she told her own.

"I stopped to write *Lucky*," she told National Public Radio's Terry Gross in July 2002. "And one of the things that was very important for me to do was to get all the facts of my own case down."

Susie Salmon tells not only her own story but also the stories of other women and girls who'd been raped and killed by Mr. Harvey. As Susie recounts these women's stories, she comes to terms with why she needs to tell her own. "Each time I told my story, I lost a bit, the smallest drop of pain."

Reading this line reminded me of the first time I

thought someone could kill me. I was still living in Haiti with Uncle Joseph and Tante Denise. When I was ten years old, an older boy—Tante Denise's godson and nephew, Joël—moved into their house after his grandmother died. Many nights, over several weeks, he would walk into the room where three other girls and I slept and would slip his hands under our nightgowns and touch our private parts. Our bunk beds were lined up near the armoire from which he needed to get a set of sheets, and before he'd pick up the sheets he would touch us. Sometimes it was one or two of us. Sometimes it was all four of us, all of us too terrified even to discuss among ourselves what was going on, all of us too afraid that he might kill us if we screamed or told anyone else.

During those moments, I would pretend that my body was no longer mine and that I had merged with the bedsheet. In the daytime, I would find certain objects to keep me from thinking about the night: self-made amulets in the form of beautiful black and brown women on toothpaste boxes. I would cut out these faces and their gleaming white teeth and I would think how lucky these bodiless women were because no one could touch them in terrible ways. These women could also shield me, I thought, by drawing me into an imaginary world where people laughed all the time and had no vulnerable flesh.

One night I dreamed that the bodiless toothpaste

women all sat around me and wept. When I woke up, I was sure they'd cried so much that their tears, and not mine, had soaked my pillow. These cut-out images would come fully alive while my body was being violated. And even though these faces were as mute as I was—at times this boy would put his hand over my mouth and I would think I was finally going to die—at least they would witness my death. Later on, as an adult, I would feel a shock of recognition reading about headless paper dolls in Toni Morrison's novel *Sula*. "When I was a little girl the heads of my paper dolls came off, and it was a long time before I discovered that my own head would not fall off if I bent my neck."

While my parents were still alive, I was afraid to write about these nights. I was afraid that it might upset them. My parents had left Haiti in the middle of a thirty-year dictatorship during which most people were being terrorized. Women and girls being raped was not all that unusual. A girl could be walking down the street—she could be on her way to school alone—and if one of the dictator's henchmen decided he liked her, he could take her. My aunt and uncle managed to protect me from street threats. Yet they were not aware that a different terror existed inside their home.

Joël's stay in the house lasted around six weeks. He was eventually kicked out by his aunt for some other reason that I wasn't aware of.

Tante Rezia was the only person I ever told about Joël. I told her a few years before she died. I was visiting her in Haiti and she told me that she'd just seen Joël on the street. He looked like a zombie, she said, like the living dead. He was hungry and she gave him some money for food.

"Remember Joël?" she asked.

I started sobbing, and maybe because I didn't want someone I loved so much to start feeling sorry for him, I told her.

When I heard that Tante Rezia had died, I kept thinking of bodiless women and headless paper dolls and how they represented another kind of death, the death of innocence for little girls, some of whom do not manage to survive.

Dying Together

I was in a supermarket in Miami's Little Haiti neighborhood with my two daughters on the afternoon of January 12, 2010, when my cell phone started ringing.

"There's been an earthquake in Haiti," a family member told me. "They're saying it's 7.0 and catastrophic."

During the drive home, I looked out the window but could barely see the brightly colored homes and storefronts of Little Haiti. Dusk comes quickly on January nights, even in Miami, and this night was no different. Still, it felt as if dark clouds had swallowed the day a lot faster than usual.

My heart was racing as I started running through, in my mind, a list of the family members and friends in Haiti I would need to get in touch with. Most of them lived in Léogâne, the epicenter of the earthquake; Carrefour; and the capital, Port-au-Prince. I tried to think of the most efficient way to find out about the greatest number of people. It would be best, I told myself, to call several people who would have news of everyone else—the family leaders, if you will. My cousin Maxo was one of those people.

At sixty-two, Maxo had been married several times and had eleven children ranging in age from forty-two years to fifteen months old. He was a lively and over-indulgent soul who'd taken over the family homestead after his father, my minister uncle, had died, in 2004. Maxo, his wife, and five of his youngest children were living in Bel Air, the hillside neighborhood where I grew up, near one of Port-au-Prince's most famous cathedrals. When I dialed Maxo's number at a red light on the way home, I heard a strange sound on the other end of the line, something like air flowing through a metal tube.

When I got home, my husband was in front of the television watching the news on CNN. The television screen showed a map of Haiti with a bull's-eye on Carrefour, where my husband's two uncles were living. There were no images yet of the actual devastation, just interviews with earthquake experts and the occasional survivor via Skype. The eyewitnesses were describing a catastrophic scene. The presidential palace and several other government buildings had collapsed. Entire neighborhoods had slid down hills. Churches, schools, and hospitals had crumbled, killing and burying countless people. Aftershocks were continuing, prompting a tsunami warning.

"It was as if the earth itself had become liquid," one survivor said, "like the ocean."

My husband and I kept dialing the phone numbers of friends and relatives in Haiti and getting no response. Instead, I got a call from the producers of CNN's *Anderson Cooper 360°*. They asked if I would come on the show.

I wasn't sure what I would say. What I was feeling was nearly indescribable. The country where I was born and had spent the first twelve years of my life, where many of my family members still lived, had been devastated. For all I knew, there were very few people left still alive. I was extremely worried about my loved ones. I was also feeling a deep sense of dread, a paralyzing fear that everything was gone, that the whole country had been destroyed.

As I sat in the satellite studio in Miami Beach, waiting to go on the show, I still hadn't heard from anyone I knew in Haiti. I felt like sobbing when Anderson Copper turned to me on the monitor and said, "Edwidge, I know you have been trying to get in touch with your family as well. Have you had any luck?"

"This is probably one of the darkest nights in our history," I managed to tell Anderson and his viewers that night.

When I returned home, the dark night continued. With daylight came the first images of the devastation. Piles of rubble were everywhere, many with both corpses and moving limbs peeking out. I cried watching a video of one trapped little boy whose arm could be seen reaching for his mother from a pancaked house. I didn't know then that my cousin Maxo and his ten-year-old son, Nozial, had already died, and that three of Maxo's other children—including the fifteen-month-old—would be trapped in the rubble for two days before being rescued by their neighbors.

Perhaps because the images of the helplessly trapped were so hard to take, a lot of the television news coverage quickly shifted to foreign-led professional rescues. The rescues provided a dramatic arc for viewers, a resolution that wasn't death. Among the stories that might have been too devastating to watch are some that my family members told me of hundreds of people who individually or in small groups kept vigil near a pile of rubble and spoke to their trapped loved ones as they slipped away, dying so close yet beyond their reach.

One of the books I took with me when I returned to Haiti twenty-three days after the earthquake was Haruki Murakami's 2002 short-story collection, *After the Quake.* The six stories in the collection take place after the Kobe earthquake, which killed more than six thousand people on January 17, 1995. I'd read *After the Quake* when it came out, when I was writing *The Dew Breaker*, a collection of linked stories about a torturer and the aftermath of his crimes, including their impact on his victims' lives. Even before the Haiti earthquake, I'd found *After the Quake*'s traumatized characters both instructive and comforting. None of us know how we might react when faced with a disaster that directly affects our lives and our communities. Would we keep our cool? Would we lose it? Would we go nuts?

Murakami's characters display a whole range of reactions, from numbness to flights of magical realism that some might consider madness or simply grief. The earthquake, though, is not the central focus of these stories; the aftershocks are. Not just the physical or geographical aftershocks, but the psychological ones as well.

In "UFO in Kushiro," the wife of Komura, an electronics salesman, suddenly leaves him after the earthquake. To keep his mind off the current state of things, Komura agrees to carry a mysterious package on a plane for a colleague. While traveling he observes:

> The morning paper was full of earthquake reports. He read it from beginning to end on the plane. The number of dead was rising. Many areas were still without water or electricity, and countless people had lost their homes. Each article reported some new tragedy, but to Komura the details seemed oddly lacking in depth.

Poems, essays, memoirs, stories, and novels can help fill depth gaps in a way that numbers and statistics can't. One person's well-described life and death can sometimes move us more than the mere mention of thousands of deaths can.

"Nothing is less sensational than pestilence," Albert Camus writes in his 1947 novel, *The Plague*. "Great misfortunes," he notes, "are monotonous." So how do we write about them without sounding overindulgent, self-righteous, self-piteous, melodramatic, sentimental, or a combination of some or all of the above? Humor, as Christopher Hitchens shows us, might be one way. Another might be the iceberg. Yet another way might be to spill one's heart all over the page. After all, death is one of life's most spectacular events, one that surpasses all existing words and deeds.

When writing about death, I remind myself of the mundaneness, even the routineness of it. People die all the time, though they are not all people I know or love. I also acknowledge that a death that moves me terribly and crushes me might not have the same effect on someone else. Empathy is not guaranteed, and hyperbole does not necessarily ensure it. I also try to stick to what the writer Brenda Ueland, in *If You Want to Write*, calls "microscopic truthfulness." "The more you wish to describe a Universal the more minutely and truthfully you must describe a Particular," she writes.

The more specifically a death and its aftermath are described, the more moving they are to me. The more I get to know the dying person on the page, the more likely I am to grieve for that person.

What is lacking in the newspaper accounts that Murakami's character Kumora reads are "Particulars," like this conversation between Junko and Mikaye, two friends and potential lovers, in another story called "Landscape with Flatiron."

> "I've never once thought how I was going to die," she [Junko] said. "I *can't* think about it. I don't even know how I'm going to *live.*"
>
> Mikaye gave a nod. "I know what you mean," he said. "But there's such a thing as a way of living that's guided by the way a person's going to die."

Later, Junko realizes that she couldn't live with Miyake, but she wouldn't mind dying with him. Eventually all of Murakami's characters—like my Haitian relatives right after the earthquake—begin living with the heightened awareness that they could die at any time, and out of that realization comes a kind of clarity of focus and an attentiveness, albeit temporary, to every single hour and every single day.

During most of the post-earthquake nights I spent in Haiti, I would sleep on the roof of the house of one of my husband's uncles in Carrefour. The two-story cement home had survived the earthquake intact. Still, I was too afraid to sleep inside the house, which I kept imagining crumbling on top of us in an even more powerful earthquake. So I lay in a sleeping bag on the roof and looked up at a sky full of stars while listening to the voices of neighbors who were also sleeping on their roofs or on the street, because they were too terrified to sleep inside what was left of their homes.

"Strange and mysterious things, though, aren't they—earthquakes?" Nimit, a tour guide, declares in a story called "Thailand." "We take it for granted that the earth beneath our feet is solid and stationary. We even talk about people being 'down to earth' or having their feet firmly planted on the ground. But suddenly one day we see that it isn't true. The earth, the boulders, that are supposed to be so solid, all of a sudden turn as mushy as liquid."

The liquefied earth makes us all liquid, evaporative. Others dying en masse, through man-made or natural disasters—earthquakes, plagues, epidemics, tsunamis, terrorist attacks, or mass killings—remind us that we might all be here one day and be gone the next.

"Living and dying are, in a sense, of equal value," Satsuki, a doctor in "Thailand," reflects.

Takatsuki, a newspaper reporter in "Honey Pie," the book's final story, no longer reacts to seeing dead bodies.

"I can see a corpse now and not feel a thing," he said. Bodies severed by trains, charred in fires, discolored with age, the bloated cadavers of the drowned, shotgun victims with brains splattered, dismembered corpses with heads and arms sawed off. "Whatever distinguishes one lump of flesh from another when we're alive, we're all the same once we're dead," he said. "Just used-up shells."

Though the (translated) language is stripped-down, Murakami's characters are never used-up shells. Some of their most profound, though not always flattering, traits are "unearthed" in these stories. No halos are placed on the heads of those who've disappeared or died. Death has not cleansed or whitewashed them in the memories of their loved ones. "The best friend a person has," Gabriel García Márquez writes in *One Hundred Years of Solitude*, "is one who has just died." Murakami's characters don't suddenly become saints or anyone's best friend because they've died. Still, Junpei, the fiction writer in "Honey Pie," and possibly a stand-in for Murakami, decides after the earthquake that he mostly wants to write about "people who dream and wait for the night to end."

Two years before *After the Quake*, Murakami published an oral history of the orchestrated sarin gas attack on the Japanese subway system on March 20, 1995, in which twelve people died and fifty were injured. This act of domestic terrorism was carried out by members of Aum Shinrikyo, a Japanese doomsday cult. *Underground: The Tokyo Gas Attack and the Japanese*

Psyche features Murakami's interviews with dozens of survivors of and witnesses to the attack.

"What I did not want," Murakami writes in the book's preface, "was a collection of disembodied voices. Perhaps it's an occupational hazard of the novelist's profession, but I am less interested in the 'big picture,' as it were, than in the concrete, irreducible humanity of each individual. . . . I wanted . . . to recognize that each person on the subway that morning had a face, a life, a family, hopes and fears, contradictions and dilemmas—and that all of these factors had a place in the drama."

Even while faced with two disasters, Murakami finds his own microscopic truthfulness.

Nearly two years after the earthquake in Port-au-Prince, some of my cousins were removing rubble from the school where my cousin Maxo had been the principal. In the process, they found human bones. Because they are not scientists and because Haitian officials had no interest in bones, it was impossible for them to trace these bones back to the bodies to which they had belonged: active, lively people who once spoke and laughed and loved. So rather than carry these bones around like some of García Márquez's characters do in early, cemetery-less Macondo, they decided to bury the bones next to my cousin Maxo's remains in our family mausoleum.

Whose bones are these? they wondered. Do they belong to the bright student who was always first in her class, to a parent with whom a teacher had an appointment? Are they the teacher's bones?

My family members and their friends were finding these bones in the rubble around the time of the ten-year anniversary of the terrorist attacks of September 11, 2001, and as I was talking to them, I couldn't stop thinking of human beings who had tried to be *un-boned* and fly. I couldn't get my mind off the men and women who'd been catapulted from or had jumped from the inferno of the World Trade Center buildings, then cut across a clear blue sky, down toward the ground. Some were alone. Some were in pairs. Some tried to make parachutes of curtains and clothes. One woman held on to her purse, perhaps thinking it might help identify her.

Dying en masse, especially on television, makes death—that most private of departures—public, national, global. No deaths were more public on September 11, 2001, than those of the so-called "jumpers," a word that many have rightfully called a misnomer, because these were certainly not the deaths these people would have chosen for themselves.

We are often told not to compare tragedies, but how can we not when we experience them in the same body and with the same mind? Past horrors give us a language, or a basis upon which to create a new language, to define new disasters. Public terrors become personalized. Those of us who saw the jumpers that day, either live at the scene or on television screens, saw a sky raining lives. Those of us who were from countries that have been, in their own way, on the edge of destruction, could now be counselors to our previously sheltered friends, but only barely. For no matter how much we immerse ourselves in communal grief, we all still carry our own private losses within us.

Watching any public disaster and the collective mourning it inspires always reminds me that acts of remembrance, like pieces of art, can also surface out of daily rituals, even interrupted ones. A place setting left unused at a dinner table. An oversize shoe into which we slip a foot. A tearstained journal in which we scribble a few words about unclaimed bones.

There is an ongoing debate about whether the great September 11 novel will ever be written. A case can be made that it has already been written, even if retroactively, even if in fragments. Though the stories collected in *After the Quake* were published in magazines and journals before September 11, some of his characters' senses of disorientation are similar to the testimonials of people who survived the terrorist attacks.

Thornton Wilder's novel *The Bridge of San Luis Rey*, published in 1927, is often cited as an ex post facto contender for a novel about September 11, or any other disaster. Set in eighteenth-century Peru, it examines the lives of five people who plunge to their deaths during a bridge collapse.

"Why did this happen to *those* five?" says Brother Juniper, a Franciscan missionary, and he decides to fully investigate the question. His quest is a lot like the persistent pursuit of all those who would write about the dead. Some more practical soul might have investigated the condition of the bridge; however, Brother Juniper decides to investigate the lives of those who plummeted from it. Why them? What kinds of lives did these people lead and what connections do they have to the larger community, and to each other, both in life and in death?

"Either we live by accident and die by accident, or we live by plan and die by plan," Brother Juniper thinks before launching into his inquiry.

In a March 6, 1928, letter to a former student who was writing a paper about his novel, Thornton Wilder wrote, "The book is supposed to be as puzzling and distressing as the news that five of your friends died in an automobile accident."

Later, in another letter to the same student, Wilder wrote:

Try adding this paragraph toward the end of your paper.

Mr. Wilder's book is on the form of a question. It is a question that we ask many times a year when we

read about accidents in the paper. The friends and rela-
tions of those who have died in accidents must often
put the question to themselves: was there some inten-
tion or meaning or reason for the fact that that particular person should die at that particular moment?

Many pieces of writing are crafted around a question, or a series of questions, that the writer is seeking
answers to. When I began writing my family memoir,
Brother, I'm Dying, I wanted to find out what it was like
for my father and uncle to spend nearly thirty years living apart from each other, one in New York and the
other in Port-au-Prince, then find themselves near death
at the same time—my father—from pulmonary fibrosis;
my uncle—while a prisoner of the United States Depart-
ment of Homeland Security, after fleeing Haiti in fear
for his life and seeking asylum in the U.S. at eighty-one
years old.

That quest led me not only to tons of current and
historical research and conversations with family members but to a lawsuit filed with the assistance of an immigrant advocacy group, Americans for Immigrant
Justice, which demanded that the U.S. government
turn over my uncle's detention and medical records.
I'm not sure I completely understood everything my
uncle and father went through at the very end, but I
tried to get as close as possible by learning as much as

I could about both their lives and their deaths. I was writing that book, I kept reminding myself, because they could not.

Many of the characters in *The Bridge of San Luis Rey* are writers. They are playwrights, scribes, letter writers, and students of literature. Perhaps this is Wilder's way of showing that writers are especially equipped to address sometimes-unanswerable questions.

In an essay published in *Vanity Fair* magazine a few weeks after the September 11 attacks, Toni Morrison wrote that she wanted to speak directly to the dead. At that time, this is all that seemed to make sense.

> Speaking of the broken and the dead is too difficult for a mouth full of blood. . . . To speak to you, the dead of September, I must not claim false intimacy or summon an overheated heart glazed just in time for a camera. I must be steady and I must be clear, knowing all the time that I have nothing to say—no words stronger than the steel that pressed you into itself; no scripture older or more elegant than the ancient atoms you have become.

At the ten-year commemoration of the September 11 attacks, then British prime minister Tony Blair read the final lines of *The Bridge of San Luis Rey* at a New York memorial service: "There is a land of the living and a land of the dead and the bridge is love, the only survival, the only meaning."

Too often we look for these "bridges" after people are gone. Perhaps, another novelist tells us, we should connect while we're still alive. Chitra Banerjee Divakaruni's 2010 novel, *One Amazing Thing*, tells the story of nine people who are trapped in the basement of an Indian consular office after an earthquake in an American city that resembles San Francisco. The nine include two consular staff members, a couple in a strained marriage, an African American soldier who immediately puts himself in charge, an older Indian Chinese woman and her granddaughter, a young Muslim man embittered by the treatment of Muslims after September 11, and a university student who's reading *The Canterbury Tales* when the earthquake happens.

"Until now death had been a cloud on a distant horizon. . . . Suddenly it loomed overhead, blotting out possibility," Divakaruni writes. As the situation worsens, the university student asks the others to share one important story from their lives, to tell each other "one amazing thing" about themselves.

Trapped in a small space with an increasing level of danger, these characters become less of a "collection of disembodied voices," as Murakami puts it, while they're telling their stories. They become Malathi, Mangalan, the Pritchetts, Cameron, Jiang, Lily, Tariq,

THE ART OF DEATH   61

and Uma. Each one has a face, a life, a family, hopes and fears, contradictions and dilemmas. Each one has a place in his or her own drama and then in the larger drama of the earthquake.

"Everyone has a story," Uma, the university student, reminds them, echoing one of Joan Didion's most cited lines from her essay "The White Album": that we tell ourselves—and perhaps each other—stories in order to live. A story, Divakaruni writes, is "sometimes greater than the person who speaks it," which is why our stories can outlive us.

Jiang, whom no one thinks can speak English until she's the first to volunteer her story, tells her grand-daughter Lily that when she was young she used to hear stories about spirits who came back to warn the living about the places they died.

"So many people must have died in this quake. Perhaps they can save us?" Lily replies.

Spirits and stories may not be able to save us, but we never stop trying to access them. Cameron, the former soldier, answers in his own way Tolstoy's question in *Confession*: *"Is there any meaning in my life that wouldn't be destroyed by the death that inevitably awaits me?"*

"How foolish humans were to travel the world in search of history," thinks Cameron. "Under my shoulder blades and over my head were the oldest histories of all: earth and sky." Both of which, we now know, are not as constant and stable as we might wish them to be. We can't plant our feet in the clouds—unless we're Susie Salmon—and there are times when we can't plant them in the ground either.

In his 1992 novel, *Mao II*, Don DeLillo considers the difficulties one novelist, Bill Gray, faces while trying to tackle massive global events in recent times. DeLillo also wrote a post–September 11 novel called *Falling Man*, which evokes the "jumpers," but *Mao II* addresses a broader range of disasters and includes an ongoing conversation about them.

The risk of post-disaster writing is that the writer's creation might pale—or fail—in comparison to the news, documents, photographs, video, and, more recently, cell phone footage.

"Years ago I used to think it was possible for a novelist to alter the inner life of the culture," Bill Gray declares. "Now bomb-makers and gunmen have taken that territory." Still, Gray, who refers to himself as a "sentence-maker," concedes that "there's a moral force in a sentence when it comes out right. It speaks the writer's will to live."

I agree. There's a heart-stopping, breathtaking, in-describable element to some sentences that even the most carefully chosen image can't match, due to the sentence's precision, specificity, clarity—or ambiguity, opacity, or mystery—rhythm, lyricism, and sometimes even shock value. The writers I discuss in this book are extraordinary sentence-makers. Since writers tend to have toiled the most on their opening sentences, consider the captivating first sentences of a few of the works I have mentioned so far.

Christopher Hitchens, *Mortality*:

I have more than once in my time woken up feeling like death. But nothing prepared me for the early morning in June when I came to consciousness feeling as if I were actually shackled to my own corpse.

Toni Morrison, *Song of Solomon*:

The North Carolina Mutual Life Insurance agent promised to fly from Mercy to the other side of Lake Superior at three o'clock. Two days before the event was to take place he tacked a note on the door of his little yellow house:

At 3:00 p.m. on Wednesday the 18th of February, 1931, I will take off from Mercy and fly away on my own wings. Please forgive me. I loved you all.

Thornton Wilder, *The Bridge of San Luis Rey*:

On Friday noon, July the twentieth, 1714, the finest bridge in all Peru broke and precipitated five travelers into the gulf below. This bridge was on the highroad between Lima and Cuzco and hundreds of persons passed over it every day.

Chitra Divakaruni, *One Amazing Thing*:

When the first rumble came, no one in the visa office, down in the basement of the Indian consulate, thought anything of it. Immersed in regret or hope or trepidation (as is usual for persons planning a major journey), they took it to be a passing cable car.

Opening sentences yank us out of our lives and into other lives. They also carefully set the stage for what's to come. They are our first opportunity to meet a writer, or character, and decide whether or not we want to spend the next few hours or days with them. They are, as many writers have said, anchors, hooks, handshakes, embraces, pickup lines, promises, and as science fiction writer William Gibson told the *Atlantic*'s Joe Fassler, "something like filing, from a blank of metal, the key for a lock that doesn't yet exist, in a door that doesn't yet exist."

"Do you know why I believe in the novel?" declares Bill Gray. "It's a democratic shout. Anybody can write a great novel, one great novel, almost any amateur off the street. . . . Some nameless drudge, some desperado with barely a nurtured dream can sit down and find his voice and luck out and do it."

I too yearn not for a singular authorative voice on any particular event or subject, or disaster, but for a chorus of voices. DeLillo's Bill Gray, Haruki Murakami, Thornton Wilder, Chitra Divakaruni, and others remain my companions while I try to describe my own version of a shattered world. Still, there will always be books like theirs. Writers will never stop writing them, because, alone or en masse, people will continue to die, and though it happens every day, when it hits close to home, we will always be caught off guard. We will always be amazed that it's touched our lives as well.

On December 17, 2012, nearly three years after the earthquake in Haiti, I was in Miami, looking at cathedrals, while others were burying their dead. It was the first day of a design competition to choose an architectural plan to rebuild Notre Dame de l'Assomption, Our Lady of the Assumption, Port-au-Prince's most famous cathedral. This cathedral was so central to the city that before it was leveled in the January 12, 2010, earthquake, its turrets could be seen from most places in the city, as well as from the sea; mariners used a light on the cupola of the church's north tower to help bring their ships into port.

The Catholic archbishop of Port-au-Prince was killed in the earthquake, along with nuns, priests, and parishioners. This is what, in part, motivated me, a non-architect and a non-Catholic—but a lover of cathedrals—to agree to join a panel of architects, engineers, and priests to help select three designs out of the one hundred and thirty-four that had been submitted.

I had also grown up in the shadow of Notre Dame de l'Assomption. I'd spent the first twelve years of my life in the poor but vibrant neighborhood that in part surrounds the cathedral. The chimes of the church's bells had guided the routines of my childhood, even my most painful days. My entire primary school was taken to Notre Dame de l'Assomption every Friday for Mass, no matter what religion we practiced individually.

Three days before we started looking at the cathedral designs in Miami, twenty-six people, twenty of them children, had been killed by a gunman at their school in Newtown, Connecticut. Earlier that day the gunman had murdered his mother; then, as the police closed in on him after the killings, he took his own life. Two of the children, children my oldest daughter's age, were being buried on the day of our meeting.

Looking at design after design, potential cathedral after potential cathedral, I thought of a reading I'd heard at one of the Masses I had attended at Notre Dame de l'Assomption as a child. A prophet, Ezekiel, finds himself in a valley filled with dried human bones. A loud voice asks him from the heavens, "Son of man, Can these bones live?" The bones then rattle and rise out of the ground, "tendons and flesh appeared on them and skin covered them. . . . breath entered them . . . they came to life and stood up on their feet—a vast army."

Ezekiel's bones, as well as the ones found by my cousins, now remind me of parts of Gabriel García Márquez's seminal novel *One Hundred Years of Solitude.* Certainly I am reminded of the part where Rebeca, the dirt-eating orphan, arrives in Macondo at the Buendía family compound, carrying her parents' bones in a canvas sack. We never learn who her parents are, only that they are *hers*, and that she is carrying their bones with her until she can bury them.

García Márquez seems to invent death in *One Hundred Years of Solitude.* The world he creates is "so recent that many things lacked names." Initially, there are no cemeteries in Macondo. The village's first residents recall the biblical Adam and Eve before their fall. Unlike Adam and Eve, though, Macondo's residents are fully aware of death before their paradise is affected by it.

When the gypsy prophet Melquíades becomes the first person to die in Macondo, he doesn't stay dead for long, bringing the notion of immortality to the village.

"He [Melquíades] really had been through death," García Márquez writes, "but he had returned because he could not bear the solitude." Death in *One Hundred*

Years of Solitude is indeed solitary, leading to an intense longing among the dead to rejoin the living. But death is also spectacular, mystical, massive, quick, and, eventually, plentiful.

A translation is as much the work of the translator as it is of the writer. García Márquez is famously known to have claimed, some say hyperbolically, that he preferred Gregory Rabassa's English translation of *One Hundred Years of Solitude* to his own Spanish original. The novel, as well as the first sentence—one of the most famous in literature—circles around Colonel Aureliano Buendía, moving in a few words between the present and the past, between memory and reality, and between life and death.

> *Muchos años después, frente al pelotón de fusilamiento, el coronel Aureliano Buendía había de recordar aquella tarde remota en que su padre lo llevó a conocer el hielo.*

> Many years later, as he faced the firing squad, Colonel Aureliano Buendía was to remember that distant afternoon when his father took him to discover ice.

This is indeed one of those first sentences that, to link William Gibson's metaphor to García Márquez's own introduction to the world of his novel, unlocks a

THE ART OF DEATH   69

door that doesn't yet exist but behind which everything has already happened and is only waiting to be revealed.

There are countless revelations in this novel, including the intimate feel of the poetic narrative language in which the book is written. However, some of the most profound and beautiful scenes involve death. There is the foreshadowed attempted execution of Colonel Aureliano Buendía, who believes "that a person doesn't die when he should but when he can." There's the actual execution of Arcadio, who, due to an interminable speech citing his endless list of charges, finds the entire affair "ridiculous."

Then there is Remedios the Beauty, ascending to heaven. Remedios the Beauty, like the Caribbean goddess of love, Oshun, whose signature color is yellow—as in the yellow flowers and butterflies that show up throughout the novel—possesses the powers of beauty, inherent sexuality, and death. Remedios the Beauty's smell tortures men even after they've died, "right down to the dust of their bones." García Márquez narrates Remedios the Beauty's ascension to heaven so matter-of-factly that he leaves no room for us to question it.

Remedios the Beauty simply rises, "waving good-bye in the midst of the flapping sheets that rose up with her, abandoning with her the environment of beetles and dahlias and passing through the air with her as four o'clock in the afternoon came to an end, and they were lost forever with her in the upper atmosphere where not even the highest-flying birds of memory could reach her."

The power of García Márquez's so-called magical realism is in embedding concrete factual details in his most fantastical descriptions, he told the writer Peter H. Stone in a 1981 *Paris Review* interview.

> That's a journalistic trick which you can also apply to literature. For example, if you say that there are elephants flying in the sky, people are not going to believe you. But if you say that there are four hundred and twenty-five elephants flying in the sky, people will probably believe you. *One Hundred Years of Solitude* is full of that sort of thing. . . . When I was writing the episode of Remedios the Beauty going to heaven, it took me a long time to make it credible. One day I went out to the garden and saw a woman who used to come to the house to do the wash and she was putting out the sheets to dry and there was a lot of wind. She was arguing with the wind not to blow the sheets away. I discovered that if I used the sheets for Remedios the Beauty, she would ascend. That's how I did it, to make it credible. The problem for every writer is credibility. Anybody can write anything so long as it's believed.

There's also the magisterial passing of the family patriarch, José Arcadio Buendía, whose death invokes a rain of yellow flowers. The next time the town finds itself in a deluge is after the massacre of the town's striking banana company workers.

García Márquez's rendering of this massacre was inspired by the December 6, 1928, massacre of United Fruit Company workers in the coastal town of Ciénaga. The workers were demanding better pay and working conditions but were branded as hoodlums, rabble-rousers, and communists. Pressured by the United States government, which threatened to invade to protect its interests in the banana trade, the conservative Colombian government sent in troops who shot down the demonstrators from the roofs of buildings around a public square. It's been estimated that somewhere between forty and two thousand people were assassinated, the confusion resulting from the government's refusal to admit that the army had killed more than a few people and that they had loaded the dead onto the banana trains and dumped their bodies into the sea. In the novel, José Arcadio Segundo will believe until his dying day that more than three thousand people died.

In his 2004 autobiography, *Living to Tell the Tale*, García Márquez explains how la Matanza de las Bananeras, or the Banana Massacre, and the silencing that followed influenced the corresponding scene in *One Hundred Years of Solitude.*

> Conformists said, in effect, that there had been no deaths. Those on the other extreme affirmed without a quaver in their voices that there had been more than a hundred, that they had been seen bleeding to death on the square, and that they were carried away in a freight train to be tossed into the ocean like rejected bananas. And so my version was lost forever at some improbable point between the two extremes. . . . I referred to the massacre with all the precision and horror that I had brought for years to its incubation in my imagination.

In the *Paris Review* interview, he said, "The massacre in the square is completely true, but while I wrote it on the basis of testimony and documents, it was never known exactly how many people were killed. I used the figure three thousand, which is obviously an exaggeration. But one of my childhood memories was watching a very, very long train leave the plantation supposedly full of bananas. There could have been three thousand dead on it, eventually to be dumped in the sea."

García Márquez's version of the Banana Massacre is described, in part, through the point of view of a child—García Márquez himself was a toddler when the massacre took place. He admits in his memoir that he wanted to write a novel from the perspective of a seven-year-old boy who had survived, but he didn't think a child narrator would have "sufficient poetic resources" to tell that story. In *One Hundred Years of Solitude*, José Arcadio Segundo guides us, along with the child, through the horror.

> The captain gave the order to fire and fourteen machine guns answered at once. But it all seemed like a farce. It was as if the machine guns had been loaded with caps, because their panting rattle could be heard and their incandescent spitting could be seen, but not the slightest reaction was perceived, not a cry, not even a sigh among the compact crowd that seemed petrified by an instantaneous invulnerability. Suddenly, on one side of the station, a cry of death tore open the enchantment: "Aaaagh, Mother."

Having someone whose mind and thoughts we already know guide us through the bloodshed is very helpful here. This allows us to feel as though we're equally in danger, or are traveling through the bowels of hell with a friend.

Time slows down in this passage to let us experience the people's incredulity at suddenly finding themselves before a firing squad. At first nothing is heard.

Then the child takes over the narration. His now "privileged position" on José Arcadio Segundo's shoulders offers him a view of the slaughter, which he sees in the child-centered visuals of waves and a dragon's tail.

> The survivors, instead of getting down, tried to go back to the small square, and the panic became a dragon's tail as one compact wave ran against another which was moving in the opposite direction, toward the other dragon's tail in the street across the way, where the machine guns were also firing without cease.

The child too must soon fully come to terms with what is happening, and abandon his innocent image of the dragon's tail. The adults must forsake their notion of a farce, and realize that the machine-gun fire is very much real. The child becomes José Arcadio Segundo's sole collaborator when no sign of the massacre remains and no one else in Macondo remembers that it has taken place. José Arcadio Segundo's other companion in grief is Mother Nature, who cries over Macondo, via torrential rains, for nearly five years.

I used to think of these scenes when I was writing about the October 1937 massacre of Haitian cane workers in the Dominican Republic in my novel *The Farming of Bones*. Dominican soldiers and civilians killed between ten to forty thousand people over the course of a few nights. Most of the victims were killed with machetes. I couldn't accurately tell the story of every dead person or every survivor, so I decided to focus on one fictional witness, Amabelle Desir, who during the time of the massacre had access to different sectors of that society while working as a housekeeper in the home of a military family. I had to count on Amabelle's singular tale, her microscopic truth, to tell a much larger story.

In *One Hundred Years of Solitude*, García Márquez tells microscopic and universal truths, then masterfully writes about death as though it were the only possible subject. Characters die alone, en masse, in wars, massacres, executions, drownings, suicides. They die from miscarriages and during childbirth, from old age—very old age—and disease and, every now and then, of natural causes. Some spend months and years dying and get sprawling death scenes. Others are simply done with in a sentence or two or in a few words. Some return from the dead as apparitions or ghosts. Others remain alive only in memory. Not even the wonders of magical realism can keep them alive forever.

In one of his final interviews, with the journalist David Streitfeld, García Márquez connected the act of writing these types of stories to his own fear of dying. "I think I write because I'm afraid of death," he admitted. "If I didn't write, I would die."

Wanting to Die

"There is but one truly serious philosophical problem, and that is suicide . . ." Albert Camus wrote in *The Myth of Sisyphus*. "In a sense, and as in melodrama, killing yourself amounts to confessing. It is confessing that life is too much for you or that you do not understand it."

Shadrack, the World War I veteran in Toni Morrison's novel *Sula*, openly acknowledges that life is indeed too much for him and the only thing he fully understands is the pull and tug of suicide; thus, he institutes National Suicide Day.

People contemplating suicide often withdraw from their neighbors. In Shadrack's case, the community is invited to join in. Shadrack makes suicide public and communal. During National Suicide Day, suicide becomes a performance, real-life community theater.

> On the third day of the new year, he walked through
> the Bottom down Carpenter's Road with a cowbell
> and a hangman's rope calling the people together.
> Telling them that this was their only chance to kill
> themselves or each other.

The people of the Bottom hold particular beliefs about death that make them receptive to Shadrack, whose biblical name alludes to his ability to survive, no matter what inferno he might be thrown into. Like the other residents of the Bottom, Shadrack doesn't believe in accidental death. Life might be accidental, but "death was deliberate." So the Bottom's residents are perfect candidates to "follow and understand this fatal game that leads from lucidity in the face of existence to flight from light," as Camus invites his readers to do. Except there is no flight from light. Rather there's flight *into* light, as in Morrison's National Book Critics Circle Award–winning third novel, *Song of Solomon*.

Song of Solomon follows the journey of Macon "Milkman" Dead III—the surname "Dead" symbolizing the erasure of his family history—as he uncovers his family lore and a spectacular instance of flight that some might interpret as suicide. The novel opens with the very public death of Robert Smith, an insurance agent, who kills himself because he hasn't held up his part of the bargain of being a member of the Seven Days, a group that avenges the deaths of black people murdered by whites.

As Robert Smith falls from the cupola of the town hospital, Pilate, Milkman's aunt, breaks into song (*O Sugarman done fly away / Sugarman done gone*), foreshadowing Milkman's future leap off the same cliff that one of his ancestors jumped off decades earlier. In both Robert Smith's and Milkman's leaps we see echoes of the stories of Africans jumping off the decks of slave ships hoping to fly back to the places they'd once called home.

Suicide was common among enslaved people who sought their freedom in the afterlife. Their deaths were more than physical cessations. They were transitions, spiritual journeys to places from their past, homes that had become idealized—in their minds. Suicide was also the most effective way of nullifying their designation as property. Showing that they could decide whether to live or die was one way of affirming their humanity.

Suicides and other forms of death cast a long shadow in Toni Morrison's novels. In *Song of Solomon*, Pilate—like Rebeca in García Márquez's *One Hundred Years of Solitude*—spends years carrying what she believes are her dead father's bones. A ghost comes to life in *Beloved*. In *Jazz*, a man murders his teenage lover. "They shoot the white girl first" is the memorable opening salvo of *Paradise*. "We courted death in order to call ourselves brave," Morrison's narrator tells us in her first novel, *The Bluest Eye*. Still, none of Morrison's seemingly suicidal characters fit into easy categories. Morrisonian deaths are too nuanced and complex.

"Dying voluntarily," Camus writes, "implies that you

have recognized, even instinctively, . . . the uselessness of suffering."

Literature thrives on suffering. What creates tension and conflict in most works of fiction is some type of *useful*, even if initially seemingly senseless, suffering. And by useful I don't mean useful to the sufferer but to the writer of the story. We put our fictional characters through the wringer so that we might write (tell others) about it. If we are too afraid to let them suffer, or even die, then we might fail. We also write of our most painful experiences hoping that bringing these horrors to light might serve some greater purpose. Our most humble, and perhaps most arrogant, wish is that our writing might help others feel less alone. Our suffering, or our characters' suffering—be it internal or external, physical or psychological—is never wasted. It often directs us somewhere, even if inevitably to death.

In Tolstoy's *Anna Karenina*, all the characters suffer in their own way. Anna Karenina's story was inspired by that of Anna Stepanovna Pirogova, the mistress of one of Tolstoy's neighbors. Pirogova threw herself under a train after being abandoned by her lover. Tolstoy is said to have gone to the train station to see her mangled body, and that image stayed with him, as did those of the other deaths he'd witnessed throughout his life.

Anna Karenina is introduced in a death scene, and exits the novel with her own. A watchman is run over by a train as she arrives in Moscow. The watchman's death is, of course, a bad omen, as is Anna Karenina's recurring dream of a peasant carrying a sack. (A sack also appears in Ivan Ilyich's dreams in *The Death of Ivan Ilyich*.) In life, as in novels, death is sometimes preceded by mysterious visions.

When my father was dying, he would tell my mother that he couldn't sleep, because he'd see shadows circling his bed. Sometimes he would even see his long-dead parents, most frequently his mother, who he said was wearing a celebratory red dress.

"They've come for him," my mother said. My father died a few days later.

The weekend before my mother died, she was sleeping an average of eighteen hours a day. One afternoon she woke up and appeared extremely alert and surprised to see me. Looking right past me, she said, "What are you doing here?" in a tone of voice I immediately recognized as the one she used to speak to my father.

The scythe-bearing, hooded grim reaper is only one manifestation of the angel of death. There are plenty of others. In *Anna Karenina*, it's a muzhik, a peasant carrying a sack, a "dirty, ugly muzhik in a peaked cap, his matted hair sticking out."

Though it is foreshadowed and ends up feeling inevitable, Anna Karenina's suicide does not proceed as she expects. Having always heard about this pivotal scene in the novel, I was surprised to see, when I actually read the book some years ago, that Anna Karenina shows some ambivalence and even repents at the end. I shouldn't have been surprised. A novelist as great as Tolstoy would not throw a woman under a train without having us suffer through the entire excruciating experience with her.

> And just at the moment when the midpoint between the two wheels came even with her, she threw the red bag aside and, drawing her head down between her shoulders, fell on her hands under the carriage, and with a light movement, as if preparing to get up again at once, sank to her knees. And in the same instant she was horrified at what she was doing. "Where am I? What am I doing? Why?" She wanted to rise, to throw herself back, but something huge and implacable pushed at her head and dragged over her. "Lord, forgive me for everything!" she said, feeling the impossibility of any struggle. A little muzhik, muttering to himself, was working over some iron. And the candle by the light of which she had been reading that book filled with anxieties, deceptions, grief and evil, flared up brighter than ever, lit up for her all that had once been in darkness, sputtered, grew dim, and went out for ever.

The moment she finds herself at eye level with the train's wheels is probably the first time Anna Karenina realizes the finality of her action, yet there is no turning back now. So she discards the red bag, as if to make herself lighter. Before that light goes out forever, though, Tolstoy fills the page with as much information as possible, some of it ambiguous. Maybe I'm wrong, but I'm interpreting the words "as if preparing to get up" as a sign that she might be changing her mind. If I were standing on the train platform and watching this scene, for example, I would see it as a clear sign that she no longer wanted to die, that she wanted to be saved and was perhaps trying to save herself.

I would find further confirmation of this when Tolstoy grabs me off the platform and places me inside her head. For just a few short sentences, Tolstoy sheds all distance offered by the third person and goes straight to Anna asking, "Where am I? What am I doing? Why?" But before she can "rise" and "throw herself back"—back in time as well, I presume—it's already too late. The train hits her head, then drags over her body, details Tolstoy might have obtained from his research about the similar death of Anna Stepanovna Pirogova.

Like Morrison's character Sula Peace, Anna Karenina gets a momentary reprieve after forsaking her struggle with death to offer some final thoughts. Hers are "Lord, forgive me for everything!" Someone else's thoughts might have involved less surrender and been more spiteful, someone who was surer about wanting to die than Anna Karenina appears to be at the end. And here we have a candle—the dying of the light—which again we might call out as an easy metaphor, except it is a candle by which Anna Karenina, a voracious reader and a writer herself, remembers or imagines reading a book, possibly an English novel. However, a more fitting read for her might have been Flaubert's *Madame Bovary*—a book also filled with torrid infidelity, betrayal, and suicide.

Tolstoy seemed to consider suicide immoral. In "Letter on Suicide," written to a friend in 1898, he told the story of a paralyzed monk who could move only his left hand. This monk lay on the floor of a monastery for thirty years and never complained, but instead maintained a "spark of life" that allowed him to inspire the thousands of people who visited him. Tolstoy closed his letter by adding, "While there is life in man, he can perfect himself and serve the Universe."

"Suicide," as author and psychiatrist Kay Redfield Jamison counters in *Night Falls Fast: Understanding Suicide*, "is not a blot on anyone's name; it is a tragedy." It is also saturated with ambivalence. As Jamison puts it, "The line between suicidal thoughts and action is not as clear as it might seem. A potentially deadly impulse may be interrupted before it is ever acted upon, or an attempt with mild intent and danger of death may be carried out in full expectation of discovery and survival."

I have written two fictional suicides in my work. The first one is in my novel *Breath, Eyes, Memory*, which I began writing when I was eighteen years old and finished when I was twenty-four. In the novel, the narrator's mother, traumatized by having been raped by a stranger in Haiti and giving birth to the narrator, Sophie, commits suicide when she becomes pregnant with a second child. The suicide happens offstage and Sophie hears about it from a telephone conversation with her mother's boyfriend. During the phone call, Sophie tries to concentrate on anything but what her mother's boyfriend is telling her, which is how my younger self imagined I might react if I were getting similar news. Sophie remains calm. The mother's boyfriend is blunt and passes on information coldly, in part because he is in shock. At this point both Sophie and the boyfriend are in shock. To convey this, I stripped down the language as much as I could, even reducing dialogue tags.

> "Is my mother in the hospital?"
> "*Non*. She is rather in the morgue."
> I admired the elegance in the way he said it. Now
> he would have to say it to my grandmother, who had

lost her daughter, and to my Tante Atie, who had lost her only sister.

"Am I hearing you right?" I asked.

"She is gone."

I was trying not to be sentimental and melodramatic, not to overdramatize the reaction to a death that already seemed over-the-top. Still, I wish now that I had included more confrontation, so that it wouldn't seem as though Sophie had immediately accepted her mother's death.

When Sophie pushes her mother's boyfriend for further details, he tells her that he woke up in the middle of the night and found her mother lying on the bathroom floor on a pile of bloody sheets. She was still alive when he found her but later dies in the hospital from her seventeen self-inflicted stab wounds.

If I were writing this novel now, I would inflict the mother with fewer stab wounds. Still, I keep thinking of Hospital Tommy saying in *Song of Solomon* that "every killing is a hard killing." A manic episode–induced suicide might be a particularly hard killing. Still, I feel guilty about the mother's death at times, as though I had conspired to murder an actual person.

The second fictional suicide scene is in a short story called "Children of the Sea" in my story collection, *Krik? Krak!* After Haiti's first democratically elected president, Jean-Bertrand Aristide, was overthrown by a coup d'état

in 1991, a military junta took over the country and insti-
tuted a reign of terror that led to thousands of people
fleeing by boat to the United States and elsewhere. Many
of these boats were intercepted by the U.S. Coast Guard,
and the Haitian men, women, and children onboard
were taken to Guantánamo Bay, in Cuba, where terrorism suspects would later be detained.

During that time, while listening to a New York–
based Haitian radio program with my mother one night,
I heard the story of a young woman who got on a boat
with her newborn baby in her arms. The baby died
during the trip, and when the young woman was told
by the others on the boat to throw the baby's body into
the sea, she did, then she jumped into the sea soon
after that. In my version of the story, the child is born
on the boat and then dies. One of the story's two narra-
tors recounts what happens next.

> She threw it overboard. I watched her face knot up
> like a thread, and then she let go. It fell in a splash,
> floated for a while, and then sank. And quickly after
> that she jumped in too. And just as the baby's head
> sank, so did hers. They went together like two bottles
> beneath a waterfall.

This story was written in epistolary form, as a series of letters being exchanged between lovers, one of
them—the one narrating above—writing from a sinking

vessel, so the quick and detail-less descriptions seemed appropriate. Though he does not initially want to reveal this in his letters, this man is writing what could possibly be his final words. He cannot afford to be pensive and detailed-oriented. He has time only for the essentials.

Looking back now, I realize that I preferred to tackle suicide from a distance. I felt it was more believable that way.

When I was writing those stories, I did not yet know anyone who had committed suicide. I would later spend two weeks teaching in the same spring workshop as a beautiful and gifted poet who would end up killing herself and her two-year-old son a few weeks after the seminar ended. Her father had committed suicide when she was a child and she'd never believed he was gone for good. When she was a little girl, she thought suicide was an illness and that her father was in a foreign country being treated for it. She expected him to come back one day. She also said that the only place she felt she truly belonged was in books.

Our two meetings had been five years apart, the first on a panel at my college alma matter and the second at the workshop. I didn't know her very well, but I enjoyed her poems, many of which addressed similar

THE ART OF DEATH   89

themes to those in my work: migration, dislocation, and sometimes death.

We were barely able to speak to each other the first time we met—there were four of us on the panel—but at the workshop we spent more time together, at meals and receptions and parties. I had recently gotten married and my husband and I were thinking about having children. The poet and I shared a few conversations about balancing children and writing. Her son was brilliant and beautiful. He drew pictures that seemed more vivid and recognizable than those the average toddler might draw. If you asked him, he'd tell you what type of art and music he liked. He knew the names of some famous musicians and painters.

"It's not easy," I remember her saying about child rearing and writing, but she did not make it sound impossible.

After she killed her son and then herself, I kept wondering if she'd been trying to confide in me about what she was going to do, by saying that being a woman writer with a small child was not easy. She might as well have been quoting from Anne Sexton's poem "The Black Art":

A woman who writes feels too much,
Those trances and portents!
As if cycles and children and islands
weren't enough . . .

Because her life had been cut short, our brief encounters expanded in my mind. Still, I tried to be careful when speaking about her to the other people who'd spent those weeks with us. They all knew her better than I did. Some were sad. Some were angry.

When a reporter who was writing a long article about the murder-suicide called to interview me, I managed to talk only about her brilliant and beautiful boy and how he had always seemed so happy. We all, students and faculty alike, always wanted to hug him. "Everyone was always reaching for him," I told the reporter, even as I replayed the poet's words in my mind: *It's not easy. It's not easy.*

Before it was disconnected, I called the cell phone number she'd given me, yearning to hear her voice. Then I worried that whoever ended up in charge of her phone might wonder why I was stalking a dead woman. Rereading her work after she died, I felt as though every one of her poems needed to be read with her final actions in mind. Wasn't each word an essential clue to solving the mystery of how both she and her son had ended up dead?

It might not have made a difference, but I now wish I'd had this verse from Nikki Giovanni's "Poets" to share with her:

Poets shouldn't commit
Suicide

That would leave the world
To those without imaginations
Or hearts

The message on her answering machine had been recorded in a soft voice. Still, there was a lilt to that voice.
She said her name, then added, "Please leave a message,"
or something to that effect. Reading her poems at the
workshop's closing evening, she'd mimicked many accents. She did accents well. She had a beautiful voice. I
longed to hear that voice. I wanted the news of her death
and of her son's death to not be true.

One of the things the students in her workshop liked
to say about her was that she encouraged them to write
freely. "Don't worry about it too much," she told them.
"Just write." In my mind I would keep hearing those
words in her voice, with her particular lilt and accent:
It's not easy. Just write.

Another summer, ten years later, an old friend of my
husband's (and a newer friend of mine) shot herself
on a Florida beach near her home. Though she'd been
open about her struggles with depression, our friend
seemed to have conquered the ghosts that haunted
her, including a brutal childhood in which she'd been
abused by people who should have loved and protected
her, people from whom she eventually distanced herself

by shedding her birth name. A Texan, she gave herself a new name that made her sound like an heir to the British throne.

Our friend was a photojournalist who'd seen, and had perhaps sought out, all types of horrors but also moments of extreme beauty during the time she'd spent visiting or living in over thirty countries. Her photographs were published in national newspapers and magazines. She loved music and art and was a mentor to many young people who wanted to be artists. Every year on Memorial Day, she hosted a party at her house that people traveled to from miles away. She was forty-seven years old when she died.

Some of her friends wondered how they could so easily have missed the pain behind her constant and vibrant smile, the agony behind her seemingly sparkling eyes. Was she good at hiding or were we terrible at seeing? I imagine her, a fervent and passionate lover of poetry, possibly quoting this brief but resolute poem, "Suicide's Note" by Langston Hughes, as a kind of explanation:

The calm,
Cool face of the river
Asked me for a kiss.

Or, in her case, the calm, cool face of the gun barrel demanded a kiss. And there's no way any of us could have gotten between her and that kiss. Some of her friends said they wished they'd been on the beach that day. They believed they could have stopped her. But we couldn't have been with her every second of every day, standing between her and the lure of that final kiss. We would never be as close to her as the edge of that gun barrel. She'd always be distant, far away, beyond our reach.

I'm not being evasive here by not mentioning names. Theirs are not fully my stories to tell. There's also no way for me to say any more about them without claiming false intimacy or without embellishment, without turning them into fiction.

Linda Gray Sexton—the daughter of the poet Anne Sexton, who committed suicide by carbon monoxide poisoning in her car at age forty-six—has written about her mother's suicide and her own suicide attempts. One of her memoirs, *Searching for Mercy Street: My Journey Back to My Mother, Anne Sexton*, began as a letter to her mother, "a personal message of mourning and celebration that meditated on our complicated life together," a life that included periods of abandonment, physical abuse, sexual impropriety—Gray Sexton writes that her mother would masturbate while pressed against her body in bed—as well as the ups and downs of living with and loving someone who is suffering from severe depression, which Gray Sexton also battled after her mother's death.

When readers asked if writing the memoir had been cathartic for her, Gray Sexton said no. "The catharsis had happened before I wrote the book, in my analyst's office. Writing it had been more like testifying, to myself as well as others, that such things had happened to me."

In her follow-up memoir, *Half in Love: Surviving the Legacy of Suicide*, Gray Sexton broaches the subject again.

> Like so many other suicides, my mother left no note of explanation as to why she poisoned herself with carbon monoxide, and like so many of the family members of successful suicides, I wanted to know, fervently, why she had done it—even though her life had been pockmarked with the attempts necessary for a final successful production, even though her trademark poetry demonstrated time and again, in one metaphor after another, the pain that drove her toward death.

One trademark poem, "Wanting to Die," was written in February 1964, when Gray Sexton was eleven years old. As if anticipating her daughter's later quest for impossible answers, Anne Sexton writes:

But suicides have a special language.
Like carpenters they want to know *which tools*.
They never ask *why build*.

In a letter to her friend Anne Clark, in which she discusses "Wanting to Die," Anne Sexton explained that she was trying to explore, among other things, "the sex of death" in that poem.

When (to me) death takes you and puts you thru [sic] the wringer, it's a man. But when you kill yourself it's a woman. And it goes on from there to this discovery that 1. I don't think the dead are dead 2. that I certainly don't think I'll die even tho [sic] I'm dead 3. that suicides go to a special place . . . asleep for instance. 4. that suicide is a form of masturbation!!!

Having met at a graduate writing workshop early in their careers, Anne Sexton and the poet and novelist Sylvia Plath were acquaintances, or at least drinking buddies. (They would go drinking after their writing seminar to keep the discussions going.) After Plath committed suicide by gassing herself in her oven with two small children nearby, Sexton wrote an elegiac poem for her.

"I think I have finished the poem for Sylvia Plath and I think it is pretty good," she wrote to the poet Robert Lowell in June 1963. "I tried to make it sound like her but, as usual, this attempt was not fruitful; the spirit of imitation did not last and now it sounds, as usual, like Sexton."

When Nicholas Hughes, a fisheries biologist and Sylvia Plath's second child, hanged himself in March 2009 at forty-seven years old, Gray Sexton penned an editorial for the *New York Times* called "A Tortured Inheritance."

"Did it surprise me to read about his suicide?" she writes. "Not in the least. . . . Nicholas Hughes's mother, and mine, succumbed to the exhaustion of unrelenting depression. They self-destructed. And we grew up in the wreckage of their catastrophe."

Both Anne Sexton and Sylvia Plath saw dying as part of their oeuvre.

In "Lady Lazarus," Plath writes,

Dying
Is an art, like everything else.
I do it exceptionally well.

In "Sylvia's Death," the poem Sexton wrote for Plath, Sexton refers to suicide, a common obsession that haunted them both, as their "boy." Sexton writes,

how did you crawl into,

crawl down alone
into the death I wanted so badly and for so long . . .

In spite of her inclination toward suicide, Anne Sexton seemed to disapprove of euthanasia and other types of killing. "I do think that killing people for any reason is perfectly terrible," she wrote to Anne Clarke. "I don't care what they did, even Hitler for instance. And I think that being killed is perfectly terrible, even dying softly in your sleep."

While on an airplane on her way to a reading, five years before she died, Anne Sexton penned a letter to her daughter that read like yet another suicide note.

"This is my message to the 40-year-old Linda. . . . Life is not easy. . . . Be your own woman. Belong to those you love. Talk to my poems, and talk to your heart— I'm in both: if you need me."

Gray Sexton would of course need more than her mother's poems. Though the poet remained alive through her poems, the mother was gone. Reflecting on her mother's letter when she is actually forty years old, Gray Sexton writes, "Mother may always talk to me from that airplane high in the sky, but finally I am able to answer her. . . . I cast my feelings into 'Language'— the shared medium in which Mother and I reveled—to find freedom."

Even though Anne Sexton is dead, both she and her daughter continue to *do* language and that, in the end, may be the measure of both their lives.

Condemned to Die

"The contrary of suicide," Albert Camus wrote in *The Myth of Sisyphus*, "in fact, is the man condemned to death."

Camus and Tolstoy felt similarly about capital punishment. In "I Cannot Be Silent," Tolstoy's response to the 1908 hanging of twenty peasants who'd revolted against their landlords, he wrote, "They arrange to do these things secretly, at daybreak, so that no one should see them done, and they arrange that the responsibility for these iniquities shall be so subdivided among those who commit them that each may think and say it is not he who is responsible for them."

My novel-in-stories, *The Dew Breaker*, is about a torturer and executioner during Haiti's Duvalier dictatorship. From the late 1950s to the 1980s, soldiers and paramilitary men and women, called *choukèt laroze* ("dew breakers"), would routinely take people to some of the country's worst prisons and torture chambers, often coming for them late at night or at dawn. Growing up in Haiti, I knew many of them as well as their victims. Some were our acquaintances and neighbors.

I wrote this book to explore what it was like to both live in a dew breaker's skin and be one of his victims.

What made these dew breakers think they had the power to condemn people to death, anyway? I wondered. If these executioners did not bring these people into this world, as my mother used to say, what made them think they could take them out of it?

When I was younger, I was a bit confused about the "bringing people into the world" part of the equation. Did this mean that an exception could be made for our parents, that they might possibly have license to kill us? Might there be a few extraordinary circumstances in which the person who'd given birth to us could also be the one to end our lives? What if your judge and executioner also happened to be your parent? This is contrary to the notion of birth itself, which brings to mind hope and a future. Our children, the cliché goes, are our future. The contrary of a future seems to be a child who is condemned to die.

"Black people love their children with a kind of obsession," the journalist and memoirist Ta-Nehisi Coates writes in *Between the World and Me*, his 2015 National Book Award–winning letter to his teenage son, Samori. The book poetically and powerfully describes Coates's upbringing and his intellectual coming-of-age as well as America's painful history of racism and white supremacy and the way all this manifests itself in the present.

"You are all we have and you come to us endangered," Coates writes to his son. "I think we would like to kill you ourselves before seeing you killed by the streets that America made."

"That is a philosophy of the disembodied," Coates admits, "of a people who control nothing, who can protect nothing, who are made to fear not just the criminals among them but the police who lord over them with all the moral authority of a protection racket."

During slavery, slave patrols were the police, and the law itself was deadly for people like Coates's ancestors and mine, who were considered property. One of the most powerful scenes in Toni Morrison's *Beloved* is the infanticide scene, in which Sethe, a former slave, kills her daughter rather than allow her to be returned to slavery. The novel circles around and hinges on one particular moment when Sethe's daughter, a toddler, becomes the ghost who haunts the book.

Sethe's story is based on that of Margaret Garner, an enslaved woman who ran away from a plantation in Kentucky and who, after slave catchers tried to take her and her family back, slit the throat of her two-year-old daughter with a butcher knife. Margaret Garner would probably have killed herself too, had she not been stopped.

In the corresponding scene in *Beloved*, four white men, like the four horsemen of the Apocalypse, come for Sethe and her family. The small posse consists of School-teacher, a sadistic slave owner, his nephew, a slave catcher, and a sheriff. The scene is written from the point of view of Schoolteacher, who runs the plantation from which Sethe has fled. A merciless and brutal man, School-teacher encourages his nephews to explore Sethe's "animal characteristics" by drinking her milk while she's lactating, milk that is intended for Sethe's baby daughter.

The infanticide scene opens broadly with the arrival of the four white men on Bluestone Road, where Sethe is now living. Based on his past experience, School-teacher speculates on what might happen next. Many fugitives make a run for it, he thinks, so he and his party must be careful. "Otherwise you ended up killing what you were paid to bring back alive."

When Schoolteacher reaches the shed where Sethe is hiding with her children, he and the others find a bloody scene that Morrison describes rather sparingly. That scene has some of the most deliberately unadorned language in an otherwise densely lyrical novel. The moment is both horrible and powerful enough, Morrison seems to be indicating, that there's no need to sensationalize it further.

The scene is so brief that readers often miss it, Morrison has said. In a 2010 video interview with the National Visionary Leadership Project, an African American history archive, she explained, "You know it all along . . . but the actual moment when it happens is so buried in the text you can barely find it."

Earlier in that same interview, Morrison confessed that it was extremely difficult to write Sethe's story. "It was very, very hard—not so much to find the language for it, that was difficult enough. But for me, in the process of writing, it is just not authentic or legitimate enough for me to look at it from the outside. You know, I always tell my students: it's not *a* black father; it's *yours*. You know, the one you know? *That* one. So if I'm going to imagine what it takes to kill your baby, then I have to put in my arms *my baby*. . . . And when that happens— and it's difficult—then the language just pares down. You don't get ornamental with that. You get very still, very clean-limbed, and very quiet, because the event itself is bigger than language."

This is what Schoolteacher and the others see in the shed where Sethe is trying to kill her children, and possibly herself:

> Inside, two boys bled in the sawdust and dirt at the feet of a nigger woman holding a blood-soaked child to her chest with one hand and an infant by the heels in the other. She did not look at them; she simply swung the baby toward the wall planks, missed and tried to connect a second time, when out of nowhere—in the ticking time the men spent staring at what there was to stare at—the old nigger boy, still mewing, ran through

the door behind them and snatched the baby from the
arc of its mother's swing.

I used to wonder why Morrison doesn't allow us to experience that scene from Sethe's point of view; then I realized that Sethe relives this moment on every other page of the novel. The aftermath of this act expands into every scene.

The scene in the shed is compressed, though not static, showing that the level of depth in some scenes has more to do with word choice, well-chosen details, imagery, syntax, tone, rhythm, and cadence, than with word volume. The scene begins concisely, though it is filled with the kind of tension that commands us not to turn away. Two boys—they are allowed to be boys, children, hurt and wounded children—are bleeding. But their mother is not yet allowed to be their mother. She is a "nigger woman" who is holding bleeding children, one of them by the heels. Then the moment that always makes me gasp, no matter how many times I've read the book, is when Sethe avoids eye contact with the slave catchers, then swings her baby against the wall, missing, then tries again "to connect."

The arc of Sethe's swing is the emotional center of that scene for me, and, indeed, the heart of the novel. The swing demands so much practicality in the very irrational moment when Sethe is trying to connect her baby's body with the wall to make sure the child dies. This is indeed a hard killing, a baby's execution, carried out through the determined "arc of its mother's swing." (Finally she is allowed to be a mother.) Sethe's purposeful and sorrowful act is embodied by the arc of that swing, the impossible choice she ends up making as well as the level of concentration required to carry it out.

One thing that struck Morrison about Margaret Garner's choices, she has said, is that Garner was not crazy, nor did she later show any remorse. In fact, it seemed that, if faced with the same circumstances, she might do it again. This is something that Morrison demonstrates with the deliberate arc of Sethe's swing. It would take struggle and effort to kill her own child, but there was something else, which in her mind was much worse: the living death that was slavery.

Garner and Sethe's choice is echoed in many enslaved people's sayings, prayers, and songs, their tales of freedom or death. "Oh freedom," many sang, "Oh freedom over me. And before I'd be a slave I'll be buried in my grave. And go home to my Lord and be free." Or as the abolitionist Harriet Tubman is reported to have said, "There's two things I've got a right to and these are Death or Liberty."

Another complex infanticide in Morrison's oeuvre is Eva Peace's killing of her son Plum in *Sula*. Like Shadrack,

Plum returns from World War I psychologically damaged. Plum has a drug addiction that leads to him stealing from his family, so Eva takes matters into her own hands.

The scene unfolds mostly from Eva's point of view, until Plum is close to dying. It too is told in pared-down prose, though it is not as spare as in Sethe's killing scene.

Eva walks into Plum's room and holds him as he babbles compliments at her. ("Mamma, you so purty. You so purty, Mamma.") She remembers when he was a little boy and how she used to hold him and rock him the same way. Then she drags herself to her kitchen on her crutches—she has a missing leg that, rumor has it, she severed to collect insurance money. She gets some kerosene that she pours over her son's body before lighting him on fire with a rolled-up newspaper.

> Now there seemed to be some kind of wet light traveling over his legs and stomach with a deeply attractive smell. It wound itself—this wet light—all about him, splashing and running into his skin. He opened his eyes and saw what he imagined was the great wing of an eagle pouring a wet lightness over him. Some kind of baptism, some kind of blessing, he thought. Everything is going to be all right, it said. Knowing that it was so he closed his eyes and sank back into the bright hole of sleep.

This scene includes more sensory details than the infanticide scene in *Beloved*. Plum is completely passive, though, showing a lack of control over his fate. We *see* the wet light of the kerosene. We *smell* it as it touches Plum's body. Morrison puts the reader in Plum's skin right before he's aflame, but, as if to absolve Eva, or to allow us to feel some empathy for her, Morrison grants Plum "snug delight" in having kerosene poured over him. Gradually we move from the more concrete act of a mother setting her son on fire to the more abstract notion of this brutal act becoming a kind of renewal, a baptism.

What is not there is a way out, a possible rescue. Plum's death is quietly violent, claustrophobic, and intimate. The scene's emotional strength comes out of that suffocating atmosphere. The fact that Plum is dying by his mother's hand makes it a transgression, yet it seems inevitable. At this point, what could save Plum is either his mother dropping her body over his or having water poured over him. The only water, though, is in Eva's memory. She remembers bathing Plum as a little boy. There are also tears, which Eva tries to lick before they reach her mouth. Even a glass of what she thinks is strawberry crush in Plum's room turns out to be blood-tainted water from Plum's drug use.

The "wet light" traveling over Plum's body is killing him, yet it feels soothing to him. He sinks into it and surrenders to it as one might sink into a baptismal pool. In fact, he sees what is happening to him, just as his mother does, as a kind of "blessing." He is being saved. Everything will be all right as long as the "bright hole of sleep" looms ahead.

"Dying was OK because it was sleep," Nell later thinks as she contemplates her own death, echoing the saying that sleep and death are brothers. Albert Camus might as well have been referring to Eva Peace when he wrote, in "Reflections on the Guillotine," that "Society assumes the right to select as if she were nature herself and to add great sufferings to the elimination as if she were a redeeming god." Yet neither Eva nor Sethe sees herself as a god, though what is most godlike about them is the magnitude of both their love and their wrath. Their love is so "thick," as Sethe's friend Paul D says of Sethe's, that it might not be survivable.

In Morrison's fictional world, death is not the worst thing that can happen to a person. Death is "anything but forgetfulness," Sethe tells herself while remembering her dead daughter and two runaway sons. "Death is a skipped meal," Sethe's surviving daughter, Denver, thinks, compared to losing the people you love. Many of Morrison's characters seem to think this way, though not all of them.

In a 1993 *Paris Review* interview with the writer Elissa Schappell, Morrison questioned Sethe's choice of killing her daughter by imagining how the daughter, who later appears as Beloved, the ghost, would feel about it.

"Beloved surely didn't think it was all that tough," Morrison told Schappell. "She thought is was lunacy. Or, more importantly, How do you know death is better for me? You've never died. How could you know?"

I don't want you to think that I am fond only of Morrison's minimalist death scenes. One of the most detailed and moving scenes I have ever read is in *Song of Solomon*. Pilate is shot by a bullet meant for her nephew Milkman. Consistent with her fearless, near-outlaw personality, Pilate laughs after she's been shot.

Here is Pilate's death scene.

> She stood up then, and it seemed to Milkman that he heard the shot after she fell. He dropped to his knees and cradled her lolling head in the crook of his arm, barking at her, "You hurt? You hurt, Pilate?"
>
> She laughed softly and he knew right away that she was reminded of the day he first met her and said the most stupid thing there was to say.
>
> The twilight had thickened and all around them it was getting dark. Milkman moved his hand over her chest and stomach, trying to find the place where she might be hit. "Pilate? You okay?" He couldn't make

out her eyes. His hand under her head was sweating like a fountain. "Pilate?"

She sighed. "Watch Reba for me." And then, "I wish I'd a knowed more people. I would of loved 'em all. If I'd a knowed more, I would a loved more."

Milkman bent low to see her face and saw darkness staining his hand. Not sweat, but blood oozing from her neck down into his cupped hand. He pressed his fingers against the skin as if to force the life back into her, back into the place it was escaping from. But that only made it flow faster. Frantically he thought of tourniquets and could even hear the rip of cloth he should have been tearing. He shifted his weight and was about to lay her down, the better to wrap her wound, when she spoke again.

"Sing," she said. "Sing a little somethin for me."

Milkman knew no songs, and had no singing voice that anybody would want to hear, but he couldn't ignore the urgency in her voice. Speaking the words without the least bit of a tune, he sang for the lady. "Sugargirl don't leave me here/ Cotton balls to choke me/ Sugargirl don't leave me here/ Buckra's arms to yoke me." The blood was not pulsing out any longer and there was something black and bubbly in her mouth. Yet when she moved her head a little to gaze at something behind his shoulder, it took a while for him to realize that she was dead. And when he did, he could not stop the worn old words from coming, louder and louder as though sheer volume would wake her. He woke only the birds, who shuddered off into the air. Milkman laid her head down on the rock. Two of the birds circled round them. One dived into the new grave and scooped something shiny in its beak before it flew away.

Now he knew why he loved her so. Without ever leaving the ground, she could fly. "There must be another one like you," he whispered to her. "There's got to be at least one more woman like you."

The "something shiny" scooped up by the birds is the snuffbox earring Pilate had been wearing until a few moments before, when she'd torn it from her ear-lobe and buried it in the ground with her father's bones. Inside the snuffbox is a piece of paper bearing Pilate's name. The flock of birds, one might say, is Pilate's larger-than-life spirit flying away.

As a witness, Milkman is as close to Pilate's sudden death as one might get. He not only watches her die but he *feels* her dying. He even tries to imagine what she's thinking. (Her smile while she is thinking about the first time they met.) Pilate in turn tries to make it easier for him to watch her die. She smiles, hiding her pain. She confesses her regrets to him, showing a rare moment of vulnerability. Then she asks him to sing to her. Allowing him to comfort her becomes her gift to him. In spite of his reluctance, he sings a modified version of the song she sings for the dying insurance salesman when she's first introduced in the novel (though he says "Sugargirl" rather than "Sugarman"). Thanks to that song, Pilate's life comes full circle at the end.

"Sugargirl don't leave me here," Milkman sings, but leave him Pilate must, as some of their ancestors had to lose each other to cotton fields ("Cotton balls to choke me") and to white enslavers' tyranny ("Buckra's arms to yoke me").

Blood stains Milkman's hands, and comes out of Pilate's mouth. He thinks of ways he might try to save her (tourniquets, etc.), but it's too late. Pilate is already dead.

Morrison doesn't share what words Milkman cries out to wake his dead aunt. (How inspired of her to allow those two a brief moment of intimacy in such a detailed scene.) However, she admits that the words are both "worn" and "old." Whatever words they are would sound worn in such circumstances anyway. And who could even remember, since this scene is from Milkman's point of view, all that we say at a moment like this, when someone unexpectedly drops dead while we too are in the line of fire?

Still, right before his own fate is decided, Milkman realizes not just the full breadth of his aunt's nature (she can fly) but also his own. He learns from her that "if you surrendered to the air, you could *ride* it."

In a 1981 interview with the literary critic Thomas LeClair in the *New Republic*, Toni Morrison spoke about how she addressed traditional and nontraditional outlaws in what she called her "village literature."

"My work bears witness and suggests who the outlaws were, who survived under what circumstances and why, what was legal in the community as opposed to what was legal outside it," she told LeClair. Unlike the outside world, beyond her village's gates, her novels' internal codes occasionally force her characters to decide who lives and who dies.

One of the most read and discussed short stories connected with capital punishment is Anton Chekhov's 1889 short story "The Bet." One night a rich banker hosts a party full of his gentleman friends, most of whom are opposed to the death penalty and believe that it should be replaced with life in prison.

The banker disagrees. He believes the death penalty is more humane. "Capital punishment kills a man at once, but lifelong imprisonment kills him slowly."

They're both immoral, concludes another guest. "The State is not God. It has not the right to take away what it cannot restore when it wants to."

A twenty-five-year-old lawyer joins the conversation.

If he had to choose between the two, he'd choose a life sentence, he says. "To live anyhow is better than not at all."

The banker decides to test this lawyer's convictions by offering him a large sum of money to remain in solitary confinement for five years. The lawyer happily takes the bet, and to prove how serious he is, he increases the number of years to fifteen. The banker doesn't think the lawyer will last more than three or four years. Voluntary confinement is even harder than the compulsory kind, he tells him. "The thought that you have the right to step out in liberty at any moment will poison your whole existence in prison."

The lawyer becomes the banker's prisoner, living on the banker's property. The first few years of confinement are difficult for the young man, but he eventually learns six languages, studies literature, history, philosophy, theology, and the sciences.

When the time comes for the lawyer to be released, the banker realizes that paying off the bet would bankrupt him, so he decides to kill his prisoner, but right before he does, he finds a note from him.

"For fifteen years I have been intently studying earthly life," the lawyer writes. "It is true I have not seen the earth nor men, but in your books I have drunk fragrant wine, I have sung songs, I have hunted stags and wild boars in the forests, have loved women. . . . Your books have given me wisdom."

If the story were to end here, we'd have the neat epiphany that being alone—by choice or by force—makes us wiser, stronger, better. However, the story does not end here.

"And I despise your books," the lawyer adds, "I despise wisdom and the blessings of this world. It is all worthless, fleeting, illusory, and deceptive, like a mirage. You may be proud, wise, and fine, but death will wipe you off the face of the earth as though you were no more than mice burrowing under the floor, and your posterity, your history, your immoral geniuses will burn or freeze together with the earthly globe."

A few hours before he is to be paid, the lawyer leaves his jail, losing the bet, not on his jailer's terms but on his own.

Though "The Bet" reads like an allegory or fable—the original title was "The Fairy Tale"—the story resists any easy conclusions about either life imprisonment or the death penalty. The circumstances of the lawyer's imprisonment are lavish compared to those of most prisoners. He eats well, drinks wine, plays the piano, and has access to an unlimited number of books. He can also leave whenever he likes.

The point of the story, though, doesn't seem to be the usual trope that your mind can be free even while your body is confined, the so-called "freest person on the cellblock" scenario. Freedom, like death, Chekhov appears to be telling us, can be defined in different ways. But as long as we are alive, freedom is possible. Still, the story is very singularly focused, down to the regretful reminiscing from the banker. There are no subplots or any other distracting events. The conflict, crisis, and resolution involve the same people. The banker's single focus, and ours too, is the young lawyer's choice.

There are few published accounts written by people who have been on death row. One of the most prolific chroniclers of that experience is Mumia Abu-Jamal. Mumia is a Philadelphia journalist and radio commentator who spent nearly thirty years on death row.

In 1981, Mumia's brother, William Cook, was stopped by police officer Daniel Faulkner in the streets of Philadelphia. Mumia arrived on the scene and was wounded by a bullet from Officer Faulkner's gun. Officer Faulkner was fatally shot. Mumia maintains his innocence, citing the presence of another shooter who fled from the scene. Officer Faulkner's family and the Fraternal Order of Police maintain that Mumia killed Officer Faulkner.

Mumia's case is a cause célèbre to many in the United States and around the world. His eloquence on many subjects, including capital punishment, makes him a good example of what is lost if a person who can still contribute his thoughts and ideas to society is put to death. Officer Faulkner's family and the Fraternal

Order of Police consider Mumia's outspokenness as a way of taunting them and degrading the deceased officer's memory.

Mumia has written several books while in prison and has given dozens of interviews addressing subjects ranging from homeschooling to terrorism. In 2014, he gave a commencement speech to Goddard College graduates from behind prison walls. His early prison writings, which began as a series of commentaries for National Public Radio, were compiled in his 1995 book, *Live from Death Row*.

The book opens with the lines "Don't tell me about the valley of the shadow of death. I live there." There's something very hip-hop about Mumia's opening declaration. It sounds like lyrics the rapper Kanye West, or, in my day, activist rapper Chuck D from the rap group Public Enemy, might have written.

In Mumia's prison, the death row inmates are placed in a concertina-wired cage called a dog pen and spend two hours a day outdoors. When their loved ones visit, they cannot touch them. A fifty-year-old inmate on Mumia's cellblock commits suicide by setting himself on fire. Another resigns himself to his fate and demands to be put to death.

America's death row inmates find it hard to muster up hope, Mumia tells us. They have no future to look forward to. At the end of their term is death.

"Much has been written and much has been said about 'life' within prison," Mumia writes in a chapter called "Spirit death." He continues, "The mind-numbing, soul-killing savage sameness that makes each day an echo of the day before, with neither thought nor hope of growth, makes prison the abode of spirit death."

In December 2011, after being moved from death row to the general prison population, Mumia wrote a letter to the death row inmates he'd left behind.

He recounts some extraordinary transformations he's witnessed, some of them comparable to what the lawyer experiences, and the banker witnesses, in Anton Chekhov's "The Bet."

"I've seen guys who couldn't draw a straight line emerge as master painters . . . I've seen guys come from near illiteracy to become fluent in foreign languages; I've met teachers who've created works of surpassing beauty and craftsmanship. . . . You are all far more than others say of you, for the spark of the infinite glows within each of you."

Many people use euphemisms when talking about capital punishment, as Albert Camus wrote in "Reflections on the Guillotine." They speak of it the way people once spoke of cancer. They whisper. Camus believed that if the idea of death truly made capital punishment a deterrent for criminals, we'd still have executions in public squares, would broadcast them on live television, or at least describe them in greater detail in newspapers. Camus quotes two doctors who were eyewitnesses to executions by guillotine:

> "The blood flows from the blood vessels at the speed of the severed carotids, then it coagulates. The muscles contract and their fibrillation is stupefying; the intestines ripple and the heart moves irregularly, incompletely, fascinatingly. The mouth puckers at certain moments in a terrible pout. It is true that in that severed head the eyes are motionless with dilated pupils; fortunately they look at nothing and, if they are devoid of the cloudiness and opalescence of the corpse, they have no motion; their transparence belongs to life, but their fixity belongs to death."

Camus describes other accounts of decapitation, in which a cheek blushes after it is slapped, even though the head is no longer attached to the body. A man who's just been beheaded answers when his name is called, or the head dies right away, but the body is still shaking at the cemetery twenty minutes later. All of this, Camus suggests—the understatements, the exaggerations, the precise medical details, as well as the executions themselves—arise out of a common and shared terror, our collective fear of death.

Some of us are so afraid to die that we make sentencing other human beings to death, and eventually killing them, the ultimate penalty. This is why the condemned person who refuses to cower before death—who does not weep before the crowd, who does not tremble before sitting in the electric chair, who refuses the blindfold, and does not plead for mercy from the firing squad, who smiles as the noose is placed around his neck, who refuses the last rites from the earthly representative of heaven, who laughs as the kindling is lit and fire engulfs her body—is seen not only as a heretic but as incorrigible and hell-bound.

Meursault, Camus's hero (or antihero) in *The Stranger*, is such a person. After being condemned to die for killing a man, Meursault realizes that each of us is born with a death sentence, anyway: that we are all condemned to die. Meursault doesn't deny his fear of death. He simply accepts it.

"Deep down," he thinks, "I knew perfectly well that it doesn't much matter whether you die at thirty or at seventy, since in either case other men and women will naturally go on living—and for thousands of years. In fact, nothing could be clearer. Whether it was now or twenty years from now, I would still be the one dying."

In "Reflections on the Guillotine," Camus seems just a bit more hopeful than Meursault. "There will be no lasting peace either in the heart of individuals or in social customs," Camus writes, "until death is outlawed."

Close Calls

Over the course of my life, I've had a few close calls, incidents that a second or a minute later might have changed my life. Or might have ended it. I have never experienced the classic near-death experience, though, the one that includes an out-of-body moment when one's spirit floats away from one's body to hover in a state of heightened awareness from the ceiling or some higher plane. I have not passed though a tunnel or seen a super bright light. I have not had a "life review," in which everything I've ever seen, done, or experienced has flashed before my eyes. I don't know what it's like to have almost died and come back, only what it's like to momentarily feel that I might possibly have come close to dying.

When I was in my midtwenties, I bought my first car, with a six-figure mileage, from a friend of my father's. I was a reluctant driver—a terrified one, really—and an overused lemon was not a good starter car for me. Once, when I was driving along a busy street in New Rochelle, New York, the car turned on its own and headed toward a garbage truck in the opposite lane. There were only a few inches between us when both the truck and my car miraculous stopped. If the garbage truck had hit me, I might have died.

A few years ago, I was standing on the landing of the steps in front of a friend's apartment in lower Manhattan. The front door was an entire story above the ground. It had snowed a few days before, then warmed up, and then the temperature had plunged again. Black ice covered both the steps and the concrete below. I'd just pulled the door shut, and had my back to the steps, when I suddenly felt myself slipping. My arms flailed and for a moment I felt as though I were flying. I somehow managed to catch the railing before free-falling all the way down. Had I plunged backward and landed headfirst on the concrete, I might have been at least brain-dead.

There was also the time soon after my mother died when I looked up from my cell phone while riding in the passenger seat of our family car and realized that my husband had accidently driven onto the wrong side of a highway ramp. Had any cars been coming off the highway at high speed, nothing could have saved us. That particular brush with death made me think of all the close calls that I and a few people I know have had over the span of a lifetime. Some of those close calls happen so quickly we barely notice them. Others are so intense that they change the way we think not just about living but about constantly being close to dying.

Every once in a while, a friend with whom I have traded such stories will send me links to "close calls" videos on YouTube. In these videos, people cluelessly walk into the paths of speeding cars, buses, and trains that somehow don't hit them. Dangers graze but don't annihilate them. In that one moment, it looks as though these people were covered with some invisible death-protection shield. Or, as my mother might have said, "It wasn't their time."

I have wanted to sit down and tally my close calls. (There have been a few others involving being caught in the middle of a police chase, a near drowning, and a dodged bullet during a drive-by shooting.) But I have been afraid to do it. What if I tempt fate by paying too much attention to it? What if becoming fully aware of the frequency of such moments makes me terrified to leave my house? What if I start wondering if my house is even safe? After all, fifty-foot sinkholes have been known to spontaneously appear in Florida living rooms.

I once sat next to a woman in a commuter turbo-prop plane, who as soon as the plane landed started thanking God at the top of her voice. At the start of the trip, this same woman had refused to change seats with another passenger who was traveling with a friend.

"This is how they'll identify my body if the plane crashes," she said apologetically, though loud enough for everyone to hear. There had been some recent crashes involving the same type of plane in different parts of the world, I later found out, so her fear was justified. Surviving a routine plane ride had seemed like a close call to her, something to be extremely grateful for having lived through. She couldn't fully trust that the plane would land and we would all walk off and go on with our lives.

She had a point. After all, don't most catastrophic events suddenly interrupt perfectly ordinary days? The "ordinary instant," Joan Didion calls it in *The Year of Magical Thinking*, her memoir about her husband's sudden death from a heart attack and the process of writing about it.

"Confronted with sudden disaster," Didion writes, "we all focus on how unremarkable the circumstances were in which the unthinkable occurred, the clear blue sky from which the plane fell, the routine errand that ended on the shoulder with the car in flames."

Unless a person is being executed, death rarely announces its exact place and time. Against the backdrop of the ordinary, it often feels abrupt, exceptional. And even if the circumstances right before death are extraordinary—if one is getting married, for example, or giving birth, or had just climbed Mount Everest— how could these otherwise-exceptional events not pale in comparison? Death always wants to hog the stage. It cannot help itself. But it does not get to hog every stage.

After all, death cannot write its own story. While we are still alive, we are the ones who get to write the story.

Among the first words Didion wrote after her husband died were *Life changes in the instant.*

The ordinary instant.

September 11, 2001, was an ordinary day in New York—until it wasn't. As was January 10, 2010, in Port-au-Prince, as was January 17, 1995, in Kobe.

Nou tout a p mache ak sèkèy nou anba bra nou, my mother had been casually saying for years. "We're all carrying our coffins with us every day." Or "We are all constantly cheating death." This is how I usually translated that Creole phrase to my mother's doctors and nurses whenever she asked me to, usually after they had tried to reassure her, during some agonizing diagnostic test or another debilitating chemotherapy session, that everything was going to be okay. *"Media vita in morte sumus,"* might have also been another suitable translation. "In the midst of life, we are in death."

The French essayist Michel de Montaigne was apparently afraid of death until he had a near-death experience of his own. One day he was thrown off his horse after colliding with another rider. He ended up unconscious for several hours and believed himself to be dying. Then, as he recovered from his accident, Montaigne realized that dying might not be so bad. He'd felt no pain, no fear. The limbo state of being alive while feeling dead is what he had found most intolerable.

"I can, for my part, think of no state so insupportable and dreadful, as to have the soul vivid and afflicted, without means to declare itself," Montaigne wrote in his essay "De L'exercitation"—translated as "Use Makes Perfect"—in which he discusses his near-death experience.

This is perhaps why we have so many tales of near-death experiences, firsthand testimonials as well as fictional accounts, whose authors are attempting to understand what it is like to exist in a body that's hovering between life and death. There's so much to imagine, so much to project onto that inexplicable void of people's medical purgatories as they swing between living and dying.

"The poets have feigned some gods who favour the deliverance of such as suffer under a languishing death," Montaigne writes. The gods of which he speaks might appear as dead relatives or heavenly figures, angels or spirit guides who offer the choice of either staying or going. Some writers, like Dante in *Inferno* have us travel through several circles of hell, if only to possibly emerge frightened but cleansed, kinder and wiser than we were before.

While medical professionals attribute these same type of visions and apparitions to neurochemicals working overtime, many of us would like near death or half dead experiences to be real because we'd love to have a second shot at life. Or we would love to see our loved ones miraculously return from the brink before it's too late. "Do not go gentle into that good night. / Rage, rage against the dying of the light."

Writing about near-death means trying to penetrate that space where death could be imminent but living still remains a possibility. Whereas death is the end of life as we know it, and as others around us are living it, having a near-death experience means someone's been given an opportunity that most other people haven't. Survivors might rightfully feel anointed. Or guilty. A few might even wish they'd died, even though their survival had seemingly required supernatural interference or assistance from faith, if not fate. Their lives should have greater meaning now than mere existence. Or should they? Maybe there's some larger mission to complete, something better to do, someone to love, or mourn.

Although it's not a typical near-death narrative, my favorite "close-call" book is Michael Ondaatje's *The English Patient*, a novel that is, among other things, about a man who escapes death only to spend the rest of his life mourning the woman he loved. Burned beyond recognition, the so-called English patient, Almásy (who is actually Hungarian), ends up in the care of a young nurse, Hana, who looks after him in an old Italian villa at the end of Word War II. Bedridden, Almásy is constantly thinking of Katharine, the married woman he fell in love with while exploring and mapping the North African desert.

The English Patient is a war novel as well as a post-war novel. Even though the war has ended, all the characters are still living with the constant likelihood of sudden death, particularly from the hidden explosives or mines that the retreating Germans have left behind. Kip, the Sikh mine sapper and Hana's lover, is the one who must dismantle those explosives, whether they're hidden under bridges, in statues, or in pianos.

Kip is constantly living in the shadow of death. The life expectancy of someone new to his job is ten weeks. Hana too has seen a lot of death as a nurse during the war. After helping Kip with one of his trickiest mines, Hana breaks down and declares:

> "I thought I was going to die. I wanted to die. And
> I thought if I was going to die I would die with you.
> Someone like you, young as I am, I saw so many
> dying near me in the last year. I didn't feel scared.
> I certainly wasn't brave just now. I thought to myself,
> We have this villa this grass, we should have lain
> down together, you in my arms, before we died."

The breathlessness of this declaration has always moved me, the shorter sentences mixed in with the longer ones, then the purposeful repetition and variations of the word "die" for even more emphasis. Reading this, I think, Whom would I want to be with before I die? Whom would I want in my arms? Or whose arms would I want to die in?

Certainly my husband's.

I would be hesitant, though, to subject my two daughters to watching me die. Would they be able to carry that memory with them for the rest of their lives? Would they be able to carry me?

Hana's declaration also brings up the inescapable link between sex and death. One way the French refer to an orgasm is as *la petite mort* or "the little death," an antidote to Freud's "death-instinct," or what he saw as our longing to self-destruct and return to our pre-existing state through war and other means. Sex would have been another way for Hana and Kip, after having just barely escaped death, to continue to circumvent *la grande mort*, "the big death," and to counter one of Freud's other notions: that we're not convinced of our own mortality and can't imagine our own deaths. (Though having watched my mother die, I can now perfectly imagine my own death.) Hana and Kip cannot escape their mortality. It confronts them every day in the devastated landscape around them, and in the dying faces of their comrades and friends.

"In a painting of his imagining the field surrounding this embrace would have been in flames," Kip thinks soon after Hana falls asleep in his arms.

Yet both Kip and Hana survive. And the English patient continues to live, even though some of his friends have died. But always shadowing the survivors of this internal and exterior war is one of Almásy's favorite words from his native Hungary, *félhomály*, "twilight," perhaps Milkman and Pilate's twilight, or the type of twilight that the French call *l'heure bleue*, "the blue hour." Maybe it's the gloaming, or what Joan Didion refers to in *Blue Nights*, her memoir of her daughter's death, from acute pancreatitis twenty months after her husband died, as "the blue of the glass on a clear day at Chartres," and that Michael Ondaatje calls "the dusk of graves."

This type of sorrow-filled dusk offers itself as an atmospheric bridge between life and death. It is the dying of the light against which we are constantly raging, the light over which death might indeed have some dominion, as it is part sunset, part nightfall, the eventide or prologue to the end. It is, as Didion writes, "the fading," so it would not be unusual for it to linger over the holiest of places, places even holier than Chartres, or Haiti's Notre Dame de l'Assomption, or any other designated holy place.

Places can be holy, Almásy reminds us, not because we are told they are, but because we want and need them to be. Places can be holy because we are sharing them with someone we love, just as some places become cursed because they've taken people we love away from us.

"It is important to die in holy places," Almásy thinks toward the end of the novel, though sometimes we must become our own holy places, roaming cathedrals, and memory mausoleums.

Circles and Circles of Sorrow

It is said that when the writer Zora Neale Hurston was a little girl, she loved a Greek myth about the wrestler Antaeus. Antaeus is the son of Poseidon, god of the seas, and Gaia, goddess of the earth. Antaeus wins all his wrestling matches as long as he remains connected to the earth and his feet are touching the ground. Only Hercules is intelligent enough to defeat him by keeping Antaeus's feet off the ground until he loses all his strength.

Both Antaeus's strengths and weaknesses must have intrigued young Zora. She might have been fascinated by the idea that being rooted or tied to the earth could empower even a god. That rootlessness could lead to defeat and possibly death might also have frightened her.

When Hurston was a child, after she'd wandered off too many times, her mother, Lucy Hurston, suspected a neighbor of having sprinkled "travel dust" on the family doorstep.

"If she had her way," Hurston writes in her autobiography, *Dust Tracks on a Road*, "she meant to raise her children to stay at home." Still, her headstrong mother encouraged her eight children to "jump at de sun." They might not land on the sun, she told them, but at least they'd get off the ground.

The contrast between Antaeus's predicament and Hurston's mother's advice must have appeared less contradictory when her mother suddenly died when she was thirteen years old. There were some beautiful African-based rituals involving death and dying in the Southern African American communities of Hurston's time.

In Hurston's community, before the dead took their last breath, pillows were to be removed from under their heads in order to make their transitions easier. Clocks and mirrors were to be covered to allow time to stand still and to stop departing spirits from seeing their reflections and staying put.

Before she died, Hurston's mother told her not to let anyone remove the pillow from under her head. She also told her not to let the clocks and mirrors be covered. But soon, in another ritual, Lucy Hurston's bed was turned around so her eyes were facing east, toward the rising sun.

"I thought that she looked at me as the head of the bed was reversed," Hurston writes. "Her mouth was slightly open, but her breathing took up so much of her strength that she could not talk. But she looked at me, or so I felt, to speak for her. She depended on me for a voice."

That voice immediately begins to both personalize and mythologize death. In order to explain death to herself, young Zora made a story out of it. That's what many of us do when the people we love die, especially, I believe, when our mothers die. Reading other daughters' accounts of their mothers' deaths, a genre that some have reductively called "momoirs"—Hurston's *Dust Tracks on a Road*, Simone de Beauvoir's *A Very Easy Death*, Mary Gordon's *Circling My Mother*, and others—I sometimes feel as though we are all the daughters of the same mythical mother. Some of us are super direct, funny. Others are pensive, inquisitive, maudlin, bitter, sarcastic, or a combination of all those things. Yet we have all been orphaned, except by our words, which we eventually turn to in order to make sense of the impossible, the unknowable.

We want to write not just of our mothers' deaths but of their lives too and of the ways, beyond the obvious, that our lives and theirs were linked. We want to share the connections that we have built with our mothers, be they through books, clothes, or words. We want to write of the disconnections too. We want to write our mothers not only as our mothers but as people, lovers, women who had a beginning that did not include us but who are now pulling us along with them into their ending. Writing, we hope, might make all this easier to grasp, even though we cannot change the outcome. While I am reading these other daughters' accounts, their mothers become my mother.

One of the ways our stories differ—aside from the singular details—is in how much our mothers suffered. My mother was mercifully gone six months after she was diagnosed with ovarian cancer. This is the way she would have wanted it. She had always said, after we'd returned from the funeral of someone who'd died suddenly, in a car accident or of a heart attack, that she would neither want to have a sudden death nor to suffer through a long illness. She wanted something in between, just enough time to put her affairs in order and get a few things off her chest. She got her wish. Not everyone gets theirs.

"The Master-Maker in His making had made Old Death," Hurston recalls thinking on the day her mother died. "Made him with big, soft feet and square toes. Made him with a face that reflects the face of all things."

On the day that we are born, our mother's face is the face that reflects all things. She is for that brief moment when they first tuck us into her arms or press her breast into our mouth, everything to us.

"Mama died at sundown and changed a world," Hurston writes. "That is, the world which had been built out of her body and her heart."

Hurston's mother's death reactivated her travel dust, and as she traveled the world, she believed her mother's ghost was shadowing her. She felt guilty most of her life that she'd been unable to keep those deathbed promises to her mother, to hold the pillow in place and to keep the clock and mirror in her room uncovered.

Another Greek myth Hurston liked was about Persephone, the goddess of springtime and queen of the underworld. When Hades, the god of death, kidnaps Persephone and takes her to the underworld, the world above dries up because Persephone's mother, Demeter, is so grief-stricken that she abandons her duties as global gardener to keep the world's plants and flowers alive. But when Persephone returns from the underworld, the world blooms again because her mother is happy. Perhaps Hurston saw in her mother, Lucy, a version of Persephone, who is so missed when she's gone that the world literally starts to die. This type of grief, as Toni Morrison writes in *Sula*, has no top and no bottom, "just circles and circles of sorrow."

A year before her death, my mother started losing weight. She gave up fatty foods and sweets and went to herbalists who sold her pills and herbs that were supposed to regulate her digestion. She was also seeing her primary physician in New York every three months.

The weight flying off seemed like a reward for good behavior. The only downside was that my mother, who now weighed less than me after two pregnancies had plumped me up, was burping all the time, as if there were thunder trapped inside her shrinking body.

At Christmastime, I invited her to come spend the holidays with me and my family in Miami. At first she said no. Her birthday was three days after Christmas and she wanted to spend it at her home in Brooklyn. She changed her mind right before Christmas and came to Miami.

On Christmas Day, she cooked a lavish dinner, of which she ate very little. She ate even less at her birthday dinner, three days later, when we took her to one of her favorite Haitian restaurants.

I took my mother to see my physician friend Rose-May right after New Year's. I spotted the alarmed look on Rose-May's face as soon as she touched my mother's stomach, which in spite of her weight loss was twice its usual size. Rose-May took my hand and guided it to a spot near my mother's protruding belly button, which felt like a well-polished rock.

Rose-May immediately started writing down a list of tests my mother would need. Each test led to another, more complicated test, and slowly both Mom and I realized we were not on a quest to disprove something bad but on an expedition to identify how bad it was.

For a long time, I would refer to it only as a mass. Not as a tumor or cancer. That is, until Rose-May got all the test results and sat my mother down and explained the stages and how cancer is not always a mass, but how it's sometimes like a blanket over organs, or like chains that trap them, and how cancer can't always be cut out but at times only minimally reduced. I thought my mother would burst into tears, but she did not. She listened attentively and nodded. Her face betrayed no trace of fright or panic. She was still.

In the car on the way home, we were both lost in a terrible silence that should have been filled with tears. At a red light, where I stopped for too long, my mother spoke up for the first time since we'd heard the news and warned, "Don't suddenly become a zombie." She was telling me not to lose my good sense, to keep my head on my shoulders.

Later I would align this moment with something I'd read long ago by Hurston. In the 1930s, while doing anthropological fieldwork in Haiti, Hurston claimed to have come in contact with an actual zombie, a woman named Felicia Felix-Mentor. She even offered a photograph as proof.

In the photo, dressed in a loose-fitting and shabby frock, Felicia Felix-Mentor has eyes that are glazed in a way that make her look blind. Her hair is closely cropped, and even though she is standing up, she looks as she might look lying in her coffin.

The supposed zombie must remain a mystery, and Felicia Felix-Mentor looks like one, haggard and lost. The zombie's inner spiritual geography has been erased by death, but the body is still forced to wander the earth. This is the kind of life and death nobody wants, a painfully eternal living death. Of this alleged zombie, Hurston writes, "How did this woman, supposedly dead for twenty-nine years, come to be wandering naked on a road?"

If my mother came wandering down a road naked twenty-nine years from now, I would still want her, I thought in the car that day. This was the first time I understood why anyone would have their loved ones frozen through cryonics or some other method, so they could be revived at some point in the future. Then again, maybe C. S. Lewis was right. Wouldn't it be awful to die and come back, only to have to die all over again? Maybe all the Larazuses of the world would have an even harder time dying than the rest of us.

According to Haitian folklore, one way zombies can be liberated from their living death is by eating salt. People who suddenly receive terrible news are also given salt, in coffee, for example, to help ward off the *sezisman*, "the shock."

When we got home from Rose-May's office that day, my mother made us each a small cup of coffee that she sprinkled with salt.

My mother's tranquility and levelheadedness remained throughout her illness. From her first chemotherapy treatment to her last, she showed a depth of faith that I'd seen only in my father, when he was dying. My mother's faith was not so much in the doctors or in the medicine but in the belief that things would turn out exactly the way they were supposed to.

"After all, hasn't God led me here so you and I can deal with this together?" she'd say.

My mother and I spent eight years apart when I was a child. Before her diagnosis, we were living in different cities, over a thousand miles away from each other. My mother and I had spent more of our lives apart than together, but she had unknowingly come to me to help her die.

I was talking to my mother when she died. She was visibly slipping away. She was no longer eating or drinking. Her skin was cool even though she complained of feeling warm.

"Open the window," she'd say, meaning the sliding-glass door next to the hospital bed she was now sleeping in at my house. The hospital bed prevented me from sleeping next to her at night, which is something I had begun to do regularly since she got sick.

Her eyes were glazed as she drifted in and out of consciousness at around one o'clock, on the afternoon she died.

"I love you," I told her over and over in Creole. "*Mwen renmen ou.*" I held her hand. I kissed her face, stroked the salt-and-pepper stubble that was left of her usually thick and wooly hair. "You're a wonderful mother," I told her.

Hearing, they say, is one of the last senses to go.

My mother smiled.

I tearfully asked her, "Mommy, can you see heaven?" She smiled again. Then she was gone.

There was no death rattle, no sudden in-breath or out-breath. She simply stopped breathing. She smiled and slipped away.

Smiling while dying is apparently not that unusual. The body tries to produce a state of euphoria to usher us out. It releases the same kinds of neurochemicals, dopamine and serotonin, that flood our brains as we are falling in love.

My mother's face stilled. Rather than tighten in rigor mortis, it seemed to relax. One of the things I had told her at the last minute, in my rush of words and tears, was to let go.

"You can let go, Manman," I said. "It's okay to let go."

She had let go. Her previously balled fists were now wide open. I lifted her hands and folded them over her chest. I reached down and closed her eyes. I was afraid they'd pop open again, but they stayed closed. I kept my face pressed against my mother's right cheek for a few minutes and cried. Then I worried that my crying was too loud for her ears. I did not allow myself any silence between that moment and calling the rest of my family to tell them that my mother had died.

The night before, I had slept on the floor next to my mother's hospital bed. My mother would sleep a deep sleep under her oxygen mask, and she would wake up every now and then and ask me in a very hoarse voice to *pran pye ya pou mwen*, to "catch her right leg," which was moving on its own, slipping over the top of the hospital bed. I couldn't sleep. That same night I heard a man wailing outside my house. I knew the man a bit. He was a mentally ill homeless man who sometimes slept in the covered bus stop next to our house. In the past, he would shout out a random word or phrase now and then in the middle of the night, but he had never howled like this before.

That night he cried nonstop like a professional mourner, what in *Sula* Toni Morrison calls "a fine cry— loud and long," the kind of cry that made me think something awful was happening to him.

I called an area policeman we knew to check up on him. The policeman came by but left him there, still wailing as though, I later thought, he had seen my mother's spirit come and go and was frightened by it. I too was seeing my mother give up the ghost, as it were, in the leg that would not stay put, in the loud groans that I hoped were not groans of pain but of annoyance and frustration. Maybe, just as women experience birth pains, my mother was having death pains.

My mother had refused painkillers at every step of her illness. She did not want to be "gaga" at the end, she said. She wanted to know what she was saying and doing until her final breath. But the morning before she died, she told me to ask the Haitian hospice nurse for some local anesthetic, like the kind they injected in her belly when she was getting the fluids extracted. Her voice was gravelly and deep, but she stressed the word *lokal*, "local anesthesia." Her fists were balled, which the nurse said indicated that she was definitely in pain. By the time the nurse got permission from her supervisor to give my mother something stronger, some morphine, my mother was already dead.

I realize I'm writing this in circles. This is the only way it makes sense to me now. "For in grief nothing 'stays put,'" C. S. Lewis writes. "One keeps on emerging from a phase, but it always recurs. Round and round. Everything repeats. Am I going in circles, or dare I hope I am on a spiral?"

Soon after my mother died, I was talking to a writer friend who told me she had a couple of stories in mind that she will be able to write only after her mother dies. I wonder what those stories will be for me now.

When my mother was sick, we had, at her request, nightly devotions, just the two of us. After everyone had gone to bed, we would sing a hymn from her French and Creole hymnbook, pray, recite the Lord's Prayer, read another verse, then go to sleep.

Mom had some favorites, the Beatitudes among them. The Beatitudes must have offered an extra dose of consolation. They were assurances, promises that were about to be fulfilled, something I imagine she'd pierce the veil of heaven to tell me about now, if she could.

In the Beatitudes, there was comfort both for her (Blessed are the pure in heart, for they will see God) and for me (Blessed are those who mourn, for they will be comforted). She still had time to purify her heart. I had a lifetime to mourn.

Most of the time, though, Mom couldn't remember what verse she had in mind for us to read. She'd recall a word or two and I'd go fishing in an online concordance for them.

"*Syèl la*," she's say in Creole, signaling that the verse was related to heaven.

When dozens of possible choices would appear, she'd ask me to pick the one closest to the top, or one we hadn't read yet. I would use different concordances, so the verses wouldn't always appear in the same order. This is how I came across Revelation 14:13 one night.

In my mother's French Bible, it reads, "*Et j'entendis du ciel une voix qui disait: Écris: Heureux dès à présent les morts qui meurent dans le Seigneur!*" Then I heard a voice from heaven say, "Write this! Blessed are the dead who die in the Lord from now on."

Revelation 14:13 was so well suited to both my work and my mother's circumstances that it seemed like a command, not just to the Apostle John, the reported author of Revelation, but also to me. "Write this," it said, though as my mother's life neared its end, I could barely sign my own name.

I started reading C. S. Lewis's *A Grief Observed* as part of my anticipatory grief. ("And grief still feels like fear. Perhaps, more strictly, like suspense. Or like waiting; just hanging about waiting for something to happen.")

Each death frames previous deaths in a different light, and even deaths to come. During the time my mother was sick, I found myself crying uncontrollably over the deaths of people I barely knew. I attended a couple of funerals, of relatives of church members, or people from my husband's past, people I'd never even met. Mid-sob, I would realize that I was imagining sitting in the front row where the family was sitting, but at my own mother's funeral. If it wasn't her coffin I was looking at, then why had I come? Then I realized that I was rehearsing, so it wouldn't hurt so much when it was my turn.

I knew that my mother's death might feel like the death of my father, whom I had not seen take his last breath. More than a decade after he died, I still miss my father as though he died only yesterday. I can start feeling sad weeks before the anniversary of his death, even without realizing the date is approaching. I still see him in the faces and postures of some of the old, skinny, dark-skinned Haitian men I run into now and then. This is what he would look like at seventy-five, I tell myself, or seventy-eight, eighty, or, now, eighty-two years old.

In the days leading up to my mother's death, I would dream of running into my father unexpectedly at cocktail parties. He would be sharply dressed in a black tuxedo and I would be wearing a retro pink ballgown that was nearly identical to my mother's bell-shaped wedding gown. My father and I would chat pleasantly about his new hobby as a cocktail-party attendant, as though this were the sole element of his new life.

"This party is better than the last one," he'd always say right before I'd wake up. Just as he did when he was alive, he would speak to me in Creole.

In my dreams of my tux-clad dad, our conversations were strictly limited to small talk about the party we were attending, a party whose purpose I could never figure out, and whose other attendees I could never make out.

"I might leave soon," he'd say. Or "Party's over soon."

In those dreams it was as though my mother didn't exist. She didn't come up in conversation or even cross my mind. I never even thought to connect the two of them. He was my father and he was at a mysterious party that I was also attending, and that was all.

Dreams are sometimes portals of grief. Later I would realize that I was dreaming *for* my mother. In the dream,

I was her. I was wearing her dress and it is even possible that I was wearing her face.

Toward the end, my mother shared only one of her final dreams with me. A new factory was opening up in lower Manhattan, and she'd gotten a call from Mary, her old factory forewoman, to come work there.

I kept reading *A Grief Observed* as my mother was hospitalized for the last time and was preparing for home hospice. One never stops hoping for a miracle, but as my mother's body whittled away, it appeared less and less likely. Without asking any questions at all, she had signed a Do Not Resuscitate order. The focus of her prayers shifted. Rather than praying for healing, she started lingering on the part of the Lord's Prayer that says, "Thy will be done," as though it was now the only necessary prayer.

Ten years before, my father had made the same transition as he was dying, from pulmonary fibrosis. His suffering—he was constantly coughing and out of breath—was a lot more visible than my mother's. No one had to ask him to rate his level of agony. It was always writ large on his skeletal face. His "Thy will be done" had also become a plea for death.

"I didn't put myself on this earth and I can't take myself out," he'd say. "But if I could . . ."

He never allowed himself to finish the thought, but we knew he wanted out.

Mom wanted out too and started to withdraw. She stopped watching television. She no longer talked on the phone. Her own voice, she said, sounded strange to her. The cancer had invaded her lungs; she was often out of breath. She no longer wanted me to read the Bible to her. It was as if the biblical tête-à-tête had now shifted inside her head, becoming a secret chat from which I was suddenly barred.

One of the tragedies of death is that it interrupts a lifelong dialogue, rendering it a monologue. Instead of talking now, my mother mostly listened. As I watched her sleeping in the hospital bed in my house one night, I tried to imagine a type of story I could tell her to keep her awake, and thus alive—a story that would never end.

When she was awake, my mother would actively listen to updates about conversations I'd had with my brothers, discussions that she knew were mostly about her.

What had I told them about her condition? she'd ask. Her latest setback? Her recent glimmer of hope?

We'd made a pact that I would always tell them the truth, I told her.

"You're the oldest," she'd say. "You must protect them." Then I knew that she was talking about more than that particular day. She was also talking about after her death.

During the last week of her life, when she was home with us, I was playing a game with my eight-year-old daughter and was carrying her on my back.

"Put that big girl down," my mother-in-law said. "You're going to hurt your spine."

My mother, who had seemed to be asleep in her hospital bed, roused to say, "Let her carry her daughter now because one day it will be her daughter who will carry her, like she is carrying me."

With my mother pulling back on her devotions, I tried to find solace in the verses and half verses she'd led me to. Reading the Bible was one more thing I'd have to do without her after she was gone. So I kept reading *A Grief Observed* as a companion to my mother's Bible verses. I read it as my mother slept. A few phrases stayed with me.

"The death of a beloved is an amputation."

That amputation has always terrified me.

"No one ever told me that grief felt so like fear."

No one told me either.

Terror should have been part of Elisabeth Kübler-Ross's grief cycle of denial, anger, bargaining, depression, and finally acceptance. After my mother died, I became terrified—frankly, I still am—that I would suddenly drop dead and leave my children motherless.

On the one-year anniversary of my mother's death, I developed her first symptoms—bloating, indigestion, gas—and they lasted for weeks. After a few tests, it was discovered that I had an infection caused by a bacteria called *H. pylori*, which I might possibly have had since childhood and which the stress of grief might have reactivated. The homeopath I went to for body talk, a kind of holistic "read" of the body, told me that my body was remembering what it was like to watch my mother die. Even after a lengthy round of antibiotics and more body talk, my symptoms subsided only after I spent half a day in bed crying on what would have been my mother's eightieth birthday.

Like Mom, C. S. Lewis's wife died from cancer.

"One never meets just Cancer, or War, or Unhappiness (or Happiness)," he writes. "One only meets each hour or moment that comes."

In the end, each moment with my mother was bringing a deeper understanding that she was slipping away from me and that heaven, her heaven, *syèl la*, was growing nearer in her sight. She had fully surrendered, but I was still flailing. Heaven did not seem like such a great place if everyone who was there had been plucked from somebody's arms. They might be blessed, those who are dead in the Lord, but what of the wretched lot of us, those they have left behind?

Lewis seemed to have had a similar thought. "If His [God's] ideas of good are so very different from ours, what He calls 'Heaven' might well be what we should call Hell."

Lewis asks his dying wife to come to him on *his* deathbed.

"Heaven would have a job to hold me," she tells him; "and as for Hell, I'd break it into bits."

Reading the Bible out of context is discouraged by all the ministers I know, but it was the only way my mother and I could read it together in the end. We only had time to zigzag through it to find what Mom wanted and needed to hear. The way we were reading it, though, led us to many comforting fragments, pockets of isolated thoughts, islands of ideas that, completely stripped of their context, perfectly suited us.

Mixing history and prophecy, Revelation, with its fiery forecasts of famines, earthquakes, plagues, and wars, is filled with apocalyptic fury. Yet it is the one book I kept returning to in the early days after my mother died. This felt odd, even to me, but I found comfort in its plethora of gloomy imagery along with its breakneck pace and dark but highly poetic language.

Like Dante's *Inferno*, it reads at times like a horror story, yet it is more digestible, though still a forceful, cautionary tale. Revelation's vision of the world's last days is so ominous and terrifying that, though I'm sure my mother had heard parts of it read in church or had listened to sermons on it, I never would have read the whole book to her. But once she was gone, I kept finding bits of it I thought she might like.

Take, for example, the twelfth verse from the twentieth chapter:

> And I saw the dead, great and small, standing
> before the throne, and books were opened. Another
> book was opened, which is the book of life.

The book of life. Not the book of death, which is somewhat hopeful. But then the rest of the book is full of death and all kinds of monsters too:

> The dragon stood on the shore of the sea. And I saw
> a beast coming out of the sea. It had ten horns and
> seven heads, with ten crowns on its horns, and on
> each head a blasphemous name. The beast I saw
> resembled a leopard, but had feet like those of a bear
> and a mouth like that of a lion.

No one writes death like the Bible writers—resurrection too. Their vivid and detailed testimonials, their visions and messianic theophany not only bring back the dead but put flesh on their long-dead, dry bones, as in Ezekiel. The writers of Ezekiel and Revelation follow the school of exuberant and energetic description. In Revelation, though, I found myself relishing the unending rollout of horrors, all of which made it seem as though my mother was lucky to have departed from a place for which this type of dystopia was, as she believed, a real and possible future.

The framing of Revelation is a central part of its narrative. It might be a more modest writer's worst nightmare (or perhaps dream gig) to be given such a tremendous task, to jot down the lyrical yet bloodcurdling visions of an incensed muse who holds the key to life and death, and who's also ordering you not to change a single word. Still, nestled in the midst of all that destruction and fire and brimstone, what Gabriel García Márquez might call "that other death which exists within death," was my mother's little glacier, her own oasis, her vision of heaven, and even more reassuring fragments I now wish I'd had a chance to share with her, places where, after the torment and terrible suffering, everything suddenly becomes peaceful, idyllic.

It turns out that Revelation has a happy ending. In the final chapters, we catch a glimpse of a brand-new heaven and a new earth where there's no more death or grief or pain, where rivers flow clear as crystal and crops bear abundant fruit, similar, one might say, to the kind of place the world becomes when Persephone returns from Hades and rejoins her mother, Demeter, again.

"All writing of the narrative kind, and perhaps all writing, is motivated, deep down, by a fear of and a fascination with mortality—by a desire to make the risky trip to the Underworld, and to bring something or someone back from the dead," the novelist Margaret Atwood writes in "Negotiating with the Dead," an essay adapted from the Empson Lectures she delivered at Cambridge University in 2000. In other words, even when we are not writing about death, we are still writing about death. After all, death is always the eventual outcome, the final conclusion of every story.

"All plots tend to move deathward," Don DeLillo writes in the voice of his professor narrator in his 1985 novel, *White Noise*. "This is the nature of plots. Political plots, terrorist plots, lovers' plots, narrative plots, plots that are part of children's games. We edge nearer death every time we plot. It is like a contract that all must sign, the plotters as well as those who are the targets of the plot."

In her 2007 memoir, *Circling My Mother*, the novelist Mary Gordon admits that she wrote about her dead mother because writing was the only way she thought she could mourn her. I have mourned my mother in many ways—mostly by sharing stories about her with family and friends—but writing about my mother is the most active way I have grieved.

The first few weeks after my mother died, I didn't want to talk to anyone but the people who'd seen her as she was dying. I was shocked by how quickly many others expected me to bounce back and rejoin the world.

"I know your mom recently passed, but . . ." or "Sorry about your mom, but . . ." would begin requests to perform tasks that were still beyond my ability to carry out. Maybe the way death folds into the most private of spaces encourages us to underestimate the shattering weight of such a devastating loss. Perhaps uninterrupted routines and the daily flow of life force us to forget that losing a loved one to death is confounding, excruciating, sometimes even unbearable. That is, until it is our turn to grieve, and no matter how many people surround us, we end up, at one point or another, feeling totally alone.

During those first few weeks after my mother died, I had to drop out of everything but my family, out of social activities and all kinds of work.

"Perhaps, for a writer, there is no such thing as simple mourning," Gordon writes.

There's no such thing as simple mourning for anyone, really, except that as writers our grief becomes woven into the fabric of our work as well as into our source material. Mary Gordon's grieving process involved visiting the paintings of the French artist Pierre Bonnard at the Metropolitan Museum of Art, paintings that she associated with her Catholic mother.

My mother would have called it sacrilegious: to say that to come to a museum is a kind of prayer. But I want to tell her: Do you see that what I am doing is a kind of prayer? Adoration, contrition, thanksgiving, supplication. I am writing about you to witness to the mystery of an impossible love. I am sorry for the exposure that this entails. I am full of gratitude for what you gave me. I am, as artists are, a suppliant— but to whom? Saying to someone, faceless, in the air: Help me set down what I see.

Help me, Manman, I want to add. Help me, please.

"What does it mean to grieve in the absence of religious culture?" the poet Elizabeth Alexander asks in *The Light of the World*, her memoir about her artist husband's sudden death from a heart attack.

I am not sure, because I have always been surrounded by some type of religious culture, but Alexander offers a clue.

"Art is certainly my religion," she writes. But there is also her family—as well as her cultural heritage, a "syncretic" black culture that blends rituals from different strands of the African diaspora. She also has gospel music (particularly Mahalia Jackson), Lucille Clifton's poems, her own poems, her deceased husband's paintings, and deities from different continents, spirit guides, and her ancestors.

"In the absence of organized religion," she writes, "faith abounds, in the form of song and art and food and strong arms." In a lecture she gave after her husband died, she elaborated, "Art tries to capture that which we know leaves us, as we move in and out of each other's lives, as we all must eventually leave this earth. Great artists know that shadow, work always against the dying light. . . . Survivors stand startled in the glaring light of loss, but bear witness."

The need to bear witness can feel almost unrelenting after a loved one has died. Still, Alexander admits to yearning for even more guidance and more rituals.

After my mother died, I tried to follow one of the rituals she had followed after her mother died, when I was a teenager. My mother had left my brothers and me in New York with my father to go to Léogâne with her sisters to attend her mother's funeral. When she came back she wore only black clothes for six months. After that she eased into lighter colors—beige and pale pastels—but she didn't wear red or any other vivid color until an entire year had gone by.

I have been wearing mostly black clothes since college. Both my parents used to joke that when they died, I wouldn't need to buy anything to wear during my official yearlong mourning period. I was trying to look thinner and, for someone with no fashion sense at all, a bit more stylish, but my parents thought I was wearing mourning clothes when I had no one yet to mourn. They thought I always looked "coffin-ready," as the scholar Cornel West refers to the way he's dressed—black suits, black scarf—since his father's death, in 1994.

"I want rules," Alexander writes in *The Light of the*

World. "I want the prayers to say every day for a year at dusk and I want them to be beautiful and meaningful."

I wanted these same kinds of rules and prayers too.

A few months after my mother died, I was asked to write a prayer for a panel I was on at the PEN World Voices Festival of International Literature in New York. I had procrastinated for as long as I could until the morning when I was supposed to send the prayer in so it could be printed in a small book that would be distributed at the event.

I grew up in a family that prayed all the time. First at my minister uncle's in Haiti. Then with my parents and brothers in Brooklyn. Yet it was hard for me to write a prayer. This is in part because I believe prayers are meant to be private, since they often reflect our most vital desires.

I used to tell myself that writing is a kind of prayer, that silence can be prayer, that even children are prayers, living and growing prayers, that love is the most powerful prayer of all. Yet the prayer I ended up writing was inspired by my mother. It is the prayer I imagined her saying in her head during her final moments on this earth, during those minutes when she couldn't speak anymore but could still hear a little bit, as she was drifting away.

My mother had a singular and wicked sense of humor,

one that's hard to convey in translation. Her type of humor was mostly for intimates, or people she'd quickly made into intimates. Her jokes were best understood by people who already knew how she spoke, who could read her body language and listen for the nuances in her speech.

When my mother was occasionally hospitalized, most of the nurses who took care of her were Haitian. My mother was hesitant to ask too much of them, but she'd joke with them in Creole. To the one nurse who always had trouble drawing her blood, she said, "It's too bad you're not like those vampires on TV who just put their teeth on someone's neck and get blood there. Maybe there's still some blood in my neck." To the one who had to extract feces from her rectum when she was impacted, she said, "For your sake, my sister, I wish I had swallowed a big piece of gold earlier today."

Listening to her cackle even as her care became more humiliating made me realize how hard she was trying to keep a part of herself intact, even though it was a side of her she rarely made public. The nurses would laugh and continue their work and my mother would laugh between occasional groans of pain, as if she never wanted the joke to end.

At my father's funeral, my mother kept whispering something under her breath. Finally, at the gravesite, I leaned over to hear what she was saying. She was muttering over and over, "*Jusqu'à ce que la mort nous sépare.*" "Until death do us part."

Later, when I asked her why she was saying that, she told me that she was reminding my father that their contract had been terminated, that she'd signed up only until one of them was dead, and that she didn't want my father to come back and bother her.

This is why I know my mother will not haunt me. She will not be a ghost, because she was afraid of ghosts. My mother once told me how in her grandparents' time, the ankles of the dead were tied with a pretty ribbon or with a rope to keep them from coming back to haunt the living. I had a feeling that she would have tied my father's ankles together if she'd been given a chance.

My mother wouldn't have been funny in English. Even though she'd lived in the United States for decades, her English sounded like that of a newly arrived immigrant. Part of it was shyness. The other part was her lack of practice. There was not much English spoken in the factories where she worked. Everyone there had come from someplace else. She was embarrassed to speak English in other settings as well. She worried that she wouldn't be understood. Her English was hesitant and inadvertently curt. She used as few words as possible, as though trying not to squander them.

I gave her a few more English words than she might

have used in this prayer. I tried to bring in her humor
too. I called my mother's prayer "A New Sky."

Dear Lord,

*Please let this be my final prayer, my very final prayer.
Let there be no more need for me to ask anything else
of you and of this shaken and troubled but beautiful
earth.*

*Let this be the last time I think of you, before we see
each other face-to-face, light-to-light, or wind-to-wind,
or sky-to-sky, or however we will be.*

*I can't wait. I can't wait to see what I will be: what colors,
what shade, what light pillar, what rainbow, what
moon bow, what sunbow, what glory, or what new sky.*

*Let me now accept all of this, as I have already accepted
this world and all that it is and has been.*

*And please let the world go on. Let the sun still rise and
set. Let the rain still fall, quiet and soft at times, and
hard at other times. Let the oceans be still or roar, as
they always have. Let the world go on as it always has,
so that my children will know that only my spark has
dimmed and not the entire world.*

Let my children remember me. Both the good and bad of me. Let them not forget one thing about me that could help them be one better woman and three better men.

Please let the pain racking my body stop. Let it stop right now. Let my lungs stop aching. Let my breath stop sounding like hammers in my ear.

Let me not say anything hateful at this final hour.

Please make my daughter stop crying.

Let it be a sunny day when they bury me.

And, please, let my children find the five hundred dollars I left in the tin can in the freezer—I should have told them about that when I still could. Don't let them throw out my good blender. All it needs is a new blade.

Okay, maybe you can make my children forget all the times I spanked them. There might not be much to be gained from that.

Let them say nice things about me at my funeral. Things I have never heard them say before, things I would never imagine them even thinking about me. Things that have nothing to do with being spanked. Don't let them go on talking for too long at the service, though. Let them stop talking when it's time.

And let them know that I have always been praying for them like this, silently, in my head. And that if it's at all possible, I will never stop praying for them, like this, silently, from somewhere else.

Please remind them that none of us have all the time we think we have in this troubled but still beautiful world.

Let them not bury me in an ugly dress.

Guide them to my good wig. (I really should have told my daughter where it was.)

Let them not be talked out of a closed coffin. I now only want you *to see my face.*

And please, please, let my children survive this. Let them survive this. For I will not be just their Manman now. I will be their light pillar, their rainbow, their moon bow, their sunbow, their glory, their new sky.

Feetfirst

I had walked the fifteen or so blocks between the Newkirk Avenue subway station and my parents' old house in East Flatbush, Brooklyn, for years, but never with such a sense of dread. It was my first trip back after my mother's death and I wanted to revisit that stretch of Avenue D that she and I had sauntered, strolled, and marched along together throughout much of my life. I wanted to see if my mother would still be walking these same streets—alone, invisibly, without me.

In the past, my mother and I had walked to the supermarket or the Laundromat. When it was warm outside and we were both feeling heavy. Or when her doctor told her that she should walk between twenty and thirty minutes a day. Other times, we walked because she wanted to talk to me.

We never fought, but we sometimes disagreed. She and I were both the silent-treatment kind and one way we dealt with our grievances was to keep them inside until we stopped thinking about them. There was a kind of fragility to our relationship. Neither one of us thought we could handle a full-blown fight, because of all the years we'd spent apart. The wrong words might have shattered us to pieces. Every moment we spent together was time being made up. I did not realize it then, but maybe she did. If we'd had a symbol, it was our feet.

There's a Haitian Creole expression, *pye poudre*, which is the equivalent of Zora Neale Hurston's travel dust. My mother's travel dust had taken her from Port-au-Prince to Brooklyn without me. During those walks with her, sometimes I would count my age in what I called my Manman years, subtracting the eight she and I had spent apart during my childhood. Eventually I would be the one who would have *pye poudre*, venturing away from my mother: going to graduate school, falling in love, getting married, moving to Miami.

When my mother was dying, I kept taking cell phone pictures of her feet—in sandals, in socks, barefoot. I took pictures of her feet with my feet lying in bed next to her, with her doctors' feet, with her lab technicians' feet. I did this sometimes to keep my head down, so she couldn't see my tears as the nurses tried to draw her blood for the thousandth time or as she was being slid through yet another diagnostic machine that looked like a coffin. But I took these pictures also to remind me of our walks.

"Let me tell you something," she would say to me during those walks: "*Ban m di w yon bagay.*" Then our walk would turn into a lecture about some issue of great concern to her: this one guy I liked whom both she and my father hated, the fact that I wasn't sleeping enough or taking better care of myself.

Back then I looked so much like my mother that people mistook pictures of her as a younger woman for pictures of me. Our bodies even moved the same way, swaying a little bit from side to side at a rhythm and pace that nearly had us colliding. I sometimes purposefully collided with her, in lieu of a hug, which would have embarrassed her.

My mother couldn't easily say "I love you," but during these walks her body said it. Out of the corner of my eye, I could see her watching out for me, for possible potholes or sudden dips in curbs. She would take the street side so she would be more vulnerable than I was to passing cars.

My mother and I were not always going to the same place. I was commuting to Barnard College, first as a student and later to work as an administrative assistant in the financial aid office. My mother was working at another factory in Manhattan, Mary having not yet come into her life. She and I would leave the house together. If we'd just missed a bus, and the "dollar cabs" that followed the bus route were full, my mother immediately started walking to the next bus stop. Sometimes we'd make it to the subway by hiking between bus stops, my mother harboring a look of worry on her face.

Winters nearly stopped our walks. But every now and then, we'd have no choice but to make the trek, our breath forming clouds in front of us. Behind that frozen mist, my mother would notice that I was wearing the wrong kind of hat, scarf, or gloves.

"My only daughter, how are you supposed to get on in this world?" she'd say. "You will feel all this cold in your bones when you're old."

Sometimes we walked in the opposite direction, not toward the subway station but away from it, stopping at the Korean grocer's to pick up some mangoes, breadfruits, avocados, and sugarcane stalks, laid out especially for the Caribbean clientele. Right before we got home, we would reach Saint Thérèse of Lisieux Catholic Church, where we'd attended funerals, including that of my mother's older brother, Uncle Justin, who died after being hit by a car in the snow when he was over eighty years old.

Across from Saint Thérèse was the Frank J. Barone Funeral Home, which had scared my brothers and me when we moved to the neighborhood. Living three houses away from the newly dead as they were waiting to be either cremated or buried used to make us walk faster when we got off the bus.

When friends came over, they would ask us if we had ever seen any ghosts.

We hadn't.

Didn't we ever have nightmares? they'd ask.

Eventually we got so used to having the dead as neighbors that we stopped thinking about it. Besides, it wasn't like living next to a cemetery. Our dead were only passing through.

But it was a kind of purgatory, another friend insisted, where the dead might be most restless.

Eventually, what bothered us most about living on the same block as a funeral home was having cars blocking our driveway during wakes. Now and then gunshots would ring outside our house as some of the mourners expressed their grief with firepower.

That day after my mother's death, crossing the street to reach the funeral home felt like treading on holy ground, in the same way that everything one has lost takes on extra meaning. Just as remembering propping up my dying mother's skeletal body against my own to give her a bath now makes me feel as though I were part of a reverse pietà.

More than once, at the beginning or the end of our walks, my mother and I had seen a hearse pull up and a gurney taken out, with a body either covered with a white sheet or wrapped in a black body bag, and pushed through the funeral home's side door. My mother would turn to me and say, "*Nou rantre tèt devan. Nou soti pye devan.*" "Most of us enter this world headfirst, then we leave it feetfirst."

She said it so often that she sometimes abbreviated the phrase: *Tèt devan. Pye devan.* Headfirst. Feetfirst.

On that walk after my mother's death, I stood outside the funeral home for I don't know how long, waiting for one of those bodies to show up. Seeing one would be a sign that my mother was still on that walk with me.

I then walked to a bench across the street and waited some more. I was also waiting in part because I knew I would eventually write about this and I wanted some type of resolution.

By then it was late afternoon, when the bodies were most likely to come, usually from hospitals, after all the paperwork had been filled out and all the arrangements had been made. Rarely did a day go by without at least one body coming through, except maybe Sundays. Sometimes there were several bodies a day. My mother and I once spotted the outline of a small child in an infant-size body bag. That day we said nothing.

Then I saw it. The hearse pulled up and parked next to the side door. Seeing my mother's body being lifted off the hospital bed in my house, then lowered into one of those black body bags had been one of the most painful moments of my life. My mother really is a body now, I thought, and only that.

I waited for the two men who were accompanying the body to come out of the Frank J. Barone hearse. I waited for them to slide the gurney out. I had seen it done so many times that I could have closed my eyes and still described what happened next.

The men wheeled the gurney with the body toward the narrow door, its wheels grating against the side-walk. One of them searched his pocket for the key and unlocked the door. Then they began to slide the body through the door. The first man disappeared inside, sup-porting what was clearly the feet. The bulge that was the head went last.

A year to the day after my mother died, I dream that I wake up shaking after realizing that I'd abandoned her in the hospice ward for a week and had completely for-gotten about her. In the dream, I jump out of bed and rush to the hospital, panicked that my mother had been buried without anyone she loved saying good-bye.

The hospice room in my dream looks a lot like the one my mother had actually stayed in, with plain white walls and a window overlooking a courtyard with a walking trail that snaked through a garden full of ce-ment benches. In my dream, when I walk into that room, I find someone who looks like my mother standing by her bed, waiting for me. She looks like she did in her coffin at her funeral: thin, though not as haggard, and with layers upon layers of dark pancake makeup on her face. In my dream, she's wearing a long black wig and a short cocktail dress with silver sequins on the front, and before I can hug her, she begins rocking herself, then starts dancing a slow, mournful dance.

As she is dancing, I realize that she doesn't recognize me. I suddenly do not recognize her either. I can't figure out who the woman I'm looking at is, but she is not my mother. So I quickly turn around and walk out of that room, without saying good-bye.

In the hallway outside the hospice room, I mumble a few words to myself about a purse.

A few months before, among my mother's things, I had found a beautiful purse. My mother was very fond of purses. She also liked church hats, but had more purses. Maybe it was because she used to make purses in the factories. In any case, she liked having purses around. Most of the handbags and purses I found in her house in New York, and that I eventually ended up giving away, had pieces of hard caramel candy tucked in the pockets along with bus fare: two dollars' worth of coins individually wrapped in paper napkins.

Out of my mother's dozens of purses, I had kept only a few and had only one on my night table. It was a seashell-shaped vintage purse covered with gray and silver beads. The two-headed metal clasp clicked loudly when you opened and closed it. The inside was lined with gold silk that had faded in some places and gotten browner in others. Inside a tiny pocket, I saw the num-

ber 2 written in black permanent marker and I realized
that this purse had cost my mother two dollars at the
Goodwill near the diagnostic center where she'd had
some of her early tests, the same Goodwill where she
and I would browse through shelves and bins searching
for such treasures.

Somehow that purse makes its way into my dream
and as I walk away from the dancing woman in the hospice ward, the woman who was not really my mother, I
begin talking to my mother about that purse.

"*Manman, sa se bous ou,*" I mutter under my breath.
Manman, this is your purse.
It is a purse inside a dream.
As if there's nothing left for it to carry,
In the real world.
But I am still carrying it.
Like I'm still carrying you.
Manman, I miss you.
Manman, I love you.
Manman, repoze.
Please rest.
Good-bye.

I would like to thank Kima Jones, who was the first person to bring *The Art of* series to my attention. Thanks also to Taiye Selasi for talking to me about her wonderful novel, *Ghana Must Go*. I am deeply grateful to doctors Rose-May Seide, Gershwin Blyden, Ronald Joseph, Hearns Charles, and Jean Philippe Austin, and to Freda Sanon, who helped me care for my mother in her last days. I am also extremely grateful to Bishop Philius Nicolas and Pastor Gregory Toussaint, pastors Chris Cassagnol, Oscar Ferville, Joseph Samuel, Samuel Nicolas, and Serge Esperance Jr., and to Madame Yolande Ferville and Mrs. Patricia Toussaint for all their support during my mother's illness.

Some parts of this book previously appeared in the following publications and have been modified and incorporated into new text for this publication.

Introduction: Writing Life

As "Significant Others" in *Sojourners*, November 2009

As "My Honorary Degree and the Factory Forewoman" in *The Brown Reader: 50 Writers Remember College Hill*, Judy Sternlight, ed. (New York: Simon & Schuster, 2014)

Living Dyingly

In *Poets & Writers*, July/August 2017

Ars Moriendi

As "Homage to a Creative Elder" in the *Nation*,
January 2013

Dying Together

As "Lòt Bò Dlo: The Other Side of the Water" in *Haiti
after the Earthquake*, Paul Farmer (New York:
PublicAffairs, 2011)

As "Flight" in the *New Yorker*, September 2011

As "House of Prayer and Dreams" in *Sojourners*,
April 2013

Circles and Circles of Sorrow

As "A Voice from Heaven" in *The Good Book: Writers
Reflect on Favorite Bible Passages*, Andrew Blauner,
ed. (New York: Simon & Schuster, 2015)

As "Travel Dust and the Magical Tracks of Zora Neale
Hurston" in *Zora Magazine*, January 2016

The prayer "A New Sky"

As "Prayer before Dying" in *PEN America: A Journal for
Writers and Readers*, issue 19

Feetfirst

As "Without Her" in the *New York Times Magazine*,
April 23, 2015

Works Referenced

Abu-Jamal, Mumia. *Live from Death Row*

———. *Writing on the Wall: Selected Prison Writings of Mumia Abu-Jamal*, edited by Johanna Fernández

Alexander, Elizabeth. *The Light of the World*

Alighieri, Dante. *Inferno*, translated by Robert Hollander and Jean Hollander

Atwood, Margaret. *Negotiating with the Dead: A Writer on Writing*

Barrie, J. M. *Peter Pan*

The Bible: New International Version (English); Louis Segond Version (French)

Camus, Albert. *The Myth of Sisyphus and Other Essays*

———. *The Plague*

———. *Resistance, Rebellion, and Death*

———. *The Stranger*

Chekhov, Anton. *Selected Stories of Anton Chekhov*, translated by Richard Pevear and Larissa Volokhonsky

Clifton, Lucille. *The Collected Poems of Lucille Clifton 1965–2010*, edited by Kevin Young and Michael S. Glaser

Coates, Ta-Nehisi. *Between the World and Me*

Danticat, Edwidge. *Breath, Eyes, Memory*

———. *Brother, I'm Dying*

———. *The Dew Breaker*

———. *The Farming of Bones*

———. *Krik? Krak!*

de Beauvoir, Simone. *A Very Easy Death*, translated by Patrick O'Brian

DeLillo, Don. *Falling Man*

———. *Mao II*

———. *White Noise*

Didion, Joan. *Blue Nights*

———. *The White Album*

———. *The Year of Magical Thinking*

Dillard, Annie. *The Writing Life*

Divakaruni, Chitra Banerjee. *One Amazing Thing*

Faulkner, William. *As I Lay Dying*

Flaubert, Gustave. *Selected Letters*

Freud, Sigmund. *Beyond the Pleasure Principle*

———. *Reflections on War and Death*

García Márquez, Gabriel. *Living to Tell the Tale*, translated by Edith Grossman

———. *One Hundred Years of Solitude*, translated by Gregory Rabassa

———. Interview with Peter H. Stone, the *Paris Review*

Gibson, William. Interview with Joe Fassler, "The First Sentence Is a Handshake," the *Atlantic* online

Giovanni, Nikki. *Chasing Utopia, A Hybrid*

Gordon, Mary. *Circling My Mother*

Hemingway, Ernest. *Death in the Afternoon*

Hitchens, Christopher. *Mortality*

Hughes, Langston. *The Collected Poems of Langston Hughes*

Hurston, Zora Neale. *Dust Tracks on a Road*

———. *Tell My Horse: Voodoo and Life in Haiti and Jamaica*

Jamison, Kay Redfield. *Night Falls Fast: Understanding Suicide*

Kübler-Ross, Elisabeth. *On Death and Dying: What the Dying Have to Teach Doctors, Nurses, Clergy and Their Own Families*

Lewis, C. S. *A Grief Observed*

Lorde, Audre. *The Cancer Journals*

Montaigne, Michel de. *The Complete Essays*, translated by Charles Cotton

Morrison, Toni. *Beloved*

———. *The Bluest Eye*

———. "The Dead of September 11," *Vanity Fair*

———. Interview with the National Visionary Leadership Project (video)

———. Interview with Thomas LeClair, "The Language Must Not Sweat," the *New Republic*

———. Interview with Elissa Schappell, the *Paris Review*

———. *Jazz*

———. the Nobel Lecture

———. *Paradise*

———. *Song of Solomon*

———. *Sula*

Murakami, Haruki. *After the Quake*

———. *Underground: The Tokyo Gas Attack and the Japanese Psyche*

Ondaatje, Michael. *The English Patient*

Plath, Sylvia. *The Collected Poems*

Sebold, Alice. *The Lovely Bones*

———. *Lucky*

———. Interview with David Mehegan, "Words to Live By," the *Boston Globe*

———. Interview with Terry Gross, *Fresh Air*

Selasi, Taiye. *Ghana Must Go*

Sexton, Anne. *The Complete Poems*

———. *A Self-Portrait in Letters*, edited by Linda Gray Sexton and Lois Ames

Sexton, Linda Gray. *Half in Love: Surviving the Legacy of Suicide*

———. *Searching for Mercy Street: My Journey Back to My Mother, Anne Sexton*

———. "A Tortured Inheritance," the *New York Times*

Sontag, Susan. *Illness as Metaphor and AIDS and Its Metaphors*

Streitfeld, David. "The Intricate Solitude of Gabriel Garcia Marquez," the *Washington Post*

Thomas, Dylan. *The Collected Poems of Dylan Thomas*

Tolstoy, Leo. *Anna Karenina*, translated by Richard Peaver and Larissa Volokhonsky

———. *The Death of Ivan Ilyich and Confession*, translated by Peter Carson

———. *Letters and Papers*, edited by J. M. Packham

Ueland, Brenda. *If You Want to Write: A Book about Art, Independence and Spirit*

West, Cornel. Interview with Andrew Goldman, "Cornel West Flunks the President," the *New York Times Magazine*

Wilder, Thornton. *The Bridge of San Luis Rey*

———. *The Selected Letters of Thornton Wilder*, edited by Robin G. Wilder and Jackson R. Bryer

EDWIDGE DANTICAT is the author of numerous books, including *Claire of the Sea Light*, a *New York Times* Notable Book of 2013; *Brother, I'm Dying*, a National Book Critics Circle Award winner and a National Book Award finalist; *Breath, Eyes, Memory*, an Oprah Book Club selection; *Krik? Krak!*, a National Book Award finalist; *The Farming of Bones*, an American Book Award winner; and *The Dew Breaker*, a PEN/Faulkner Award finalist and winner of the inaugural Story Prize. The recipient of a MacArthur Fellowship, she has been published in the *New Yorker*, the *New York Times*, and elsewhere.

This book is made possible through a partnership with the College of Saint Benedict, and honors the legacy of S. Mariella Gable, a distinguished teacher at the College.

Previous titles in this series include:

Loverboy by Victoria Redel

The House on Eccles Road by Judith Kitchen

One Vacant Chair by Joe Coomer

The Weatherman by Clint McCown

Collected Poems by Jane Kenyon

Variations on the Theme of an African Dictatorship by Nuruddin Farah:

    Sweet and Sour Milk

    Sardines

    Close Sesame

Duende by Tracy K. Smith

All of It Singing: New and Selected Poems by Linda Gregg

The Art of Syntax: Rhythm of Thought, Rhythm of Song by Ellen Bryant Voigt

How to Escape from a Leper Colony by Tiphanie Yanique

One Day I Will Write About This Place by Binyavanga Wainaina

The Convert: A Tale of Exile and Extremism by Deborah Baker

On Sal Mal Lane by Ru Freeman

Citizen: An American Lyric by Claudia Rankine

On Immunity: An Inoculation by Eula Biss

Cinder: New and Selected Poems by Susan Stewart

Support for this series has been provided by the Manitou Fund as part of the Warner Reading Program.

The text of *The Art of Death* is set in Warnock Pro, a typeface designed by Robert Slimbach for Adobe Systems in 2000. Book design by Wendy Holdman. Composition by Bookmobile Design & Digital Publisher Services, Minneapolis, Minnesota. Manufactured by Versa Press on acid-free, 30 percent postconsumer wastepaper.